THE LEAD MINES

THE LEAD MINES:

Ballycorus and Glendalough
in the nineteenth century

Rob Goodbody

Word_well_

First published in 2023
Wordwell Ltd
Unit 9, 78 Furze Road,
Sandyford Industrial Estate,
Dublin 18
www.wordwellbooks.com

Cover image: Ballycorus lead works chimney.

ISBN: 978-1-913934-87-3 (Paperback)
ISBN: 978-1-913934-94-1 (Ebook)

British Library Cataloguing-in-Publication Data.
A catalogue record for this book is available from the British Library.

Typeset in Ireland by Wordwell Ltd
Copy-editor: Emer Condit
Cover design and artwork: Wordwell Ltd
Printed by: SprintPrint, Dublin.

CONTENTS

INTRODUCTION

Ballycorus is a townland about 2.5km to the west of Shankill, Co. Dublin. It is most notable for the chimney that stands at its highest point and is a prominent local landmark, visible from a significant distance. The hillside below the chimney bears the marks of nineteenth-century mining activity, while at the bottom of the hill is a former lead-smelting works. Most of the lead that was smelted there was not mined locally at Ballycorus but was brought from mines in the Glendalough area, some 30km to the south.

The title of this book seems to ignore the all-important lead-smelting works at Ballycorus in favour of the mines that were only a minor part of the story. This, however, is the term used locally and even the chimney, which had little or nothing to do with mining, tends to be called the Lead Mines Chimney.

This book has taken a long time to produce. Like many people from the Dún Laoghaire–Rathdown area, I knew Ballycorus and its enigmatic character from childhood, when we went there for Sunday walks. It was in the nine years from 1985, when I was secretary of the Rathmichael Historical Society, that I became aware of the lack of any decent history of the Ballycorus lead mines and lead works. By far the most numerous queries we received from members of the society and from the general public related to Ballycorus. It was also in 1985 that the local historian Kathleen Turner died and the notes that she had made on Ballycorus became available to the society. It was not much but it was a beginning, and I started to research the subject in order to fill the gap by writing a history of the mines.

Reality intervened, however, in the form of family responsibilities, the day job, and research and writings on other topics. In the early 1990s I was working on a project with William Dick, whose knowledge of Ballycorus and of industrial heritage in general was already known to me and was a source of inspiration. I suggested to him that we could co-author a book on Ballycorus, and with that in mind I began to commit the narrative to paper. William didn't take up the challenge and I diverted my energies into the production of my first book, *On the Borders of the Pale*, published in 1993 and laid out and printed by the Central Remedial Clinic Training Unit. In a flash of enthusiasm, I booked time with the Training Unit for the production of the book on Ballycorus.

It didn't happen. I got quite a bit done before it became evident that I was not going to have it ready by the date at which I had undertaken to submit it for printing. By chance I was approached at this time by Elizabeth Newsom, who had a friend who wanted to publish a book. The friend was Hazel P. Smyth, who had published a history of Booterstown in 1971 and wanted to update it and republish it. This was my opportunity to deliver a book to the CRC Training Unit and I took it on enthusiastically. I totally recast Hazel's original book, incorporating the research that she had carried out since 1971 and adding a few bits of my own; this book, *The Town of the Road—the Story of Booterstown* was published in 1994.

The following year, 1995, was the beginning of the commemorations of the 150th anniversary of the Famine and I was asked to write a short booklet on Quaker relief during that era. This diverted me away from Ballycorus again, particularly as I produced my own short book on the subject in 1995 as well as a number of articles on the topic.

The intention to finish the book on Ballycorus came to life again towards the end of 1995, when I was invited to join a steering group with a view to establishing a society devoted to mining heritage in Ireland. Here I met people with tremendous knowledge and enthusiasm for the subject and who encouraged and inspired me with my Ballycorus project. I am eternally grateful for their support—Des Cowman, Martin Critchley, John Morris, Matthew Parkes, Nigel Monaghan and others. This steering group resulted in the foundation of what is now the Mining Heritage Trust of Ireland (MHTI), and this brought me into contact with an even wider circle of inspiring people, including a number who frequently travelled over from Britain for events run by the MHTI. One of these was Stuart Chester, who would turn up on my doorstep from time to time with photocopies of material relating to lead-mining in Wicklow—and he rarely accepted an invitation to step inside the door for a cup of coffee.

One major issue that resulted from interaction with the MHTI was the overwhelming opinion that a book on Ballycorus would be incomplete without addressing the lead-mining in the Glendalough area, as the two were inextricably intertwined. This was an obvious point that I had completely missed and the manuscript, such as it was, had to go on the back burner while I undertook further research. I did a lot of that over the next while but only a little writing, and gradually the project took a back seat to other things.

My apologies to all in the MHTI that this book is not as detailed or as technical as it could be. I set out to write for a general audience—those who were contacting the Rathmichael Historical Society for information—rather than for the reader who is already familiar with the technical details of the mining and smelting industries. There is certainly scope for a larger, more detailed and more technical volume on Ballycorus and the lead mines of the Glendalough area.

In the meantime, other people contributed to the project. In

1997 I received a phone call from Dr Heinz J. Sprenger in Munich, who was researching shot towers, and we exchanged a great deal of information on the subject.

After that the partly written book and its research notes languished for a long time until finally my friends in the Rathmichael Historical Society encouraged me to get back to it and finish the job. In particular, Adrienne Hume has been instrumental in persuading me to give it attention and she also read a draft of the book, offering valuable suggestions for improvement. The day job has prevented me from giving it the time it needed, so three Christmas/New Year breaks have been spent in knocking it into shape.

Over time many other people have been of great help. One of my colleagues in Dublin County Council in the 1980s was Larry Dunne from Ballycorus, who provided copies of old photographs of the lead works and gave me access to information collected by his family. The late Howard McConnell of McConnell's Coatings, which now occupies the former lead works, was always welcoming at any time when I arrived to have another look at the works, and his background knowledge of the building complex was invaluable. Tennant McConnell has also been very helpful and accommodating. Ingrid McIlwaine, another former denizen of Ballycorus, was always happy to share her memories of the locality, while Liam and Helen Lonergan provided access to their house and shared their accumulated knowledge of the lead mines and works.

Other significant contributions and assistance have been provided by Joan Kavanagh, Robbie Carter and the former miners from Glendasan, Ian Cantwell, Ian Booth, David Bick, Dr Craig Meskell, Jonny and Thérèse O'Brien and, as always, the committee and members of the Rathmichael Historical Society.

Needless to say, my family has been with me all through this—particularly Ingrid, supportive as always, plus Aisling, Rory and

Ailbhe, who have grown up with this project bubbling away in the background. Ailbhe is now a mining journalist and has provided useful comments on the text.

As this book has been worked on for more than thirty years there must be people who have given me help or advice that I have not mentioned above. To them I can only apologise.

I should also explain the scope of the book, which is to recount the stories of the lead mines and lead works at Ballycorus, as well as the lead mines in the Glendalough and Glendasan areas of County Wicklow. It is not an inventory of the mine workings at either location. It does not include a social history of the mining communities, their houses, their social gatherings, their medical issues and life expectancies, and these are subjects I leave to others. Many descendants of those communities are still around, often still in or near the original locations, and they have stories to tell about Fiddlers' Row in Glendasan or the Ballycorus Band. I look forward to reading those accounts when someone else has committed them to print.

SAFETY WARNING

Finally, I should say that while there are extensive mine workings, buildings and other remnants of the lead-mining and processing industry in Glendalough, Glendasan and Ballycorus, anyone visiting these sites should do so with extreme caution. Some mine shafts and other mine workings are still open at Glendalough and Glendasan; others, including those at Ballycorus, have been capped, but no one knows with what they are capped or whether the capping is rotten and liable to collapse. Similarly, many of the ruined buildings are in a very poor state, including the long flue at Ballycorus, and should be viewed from a respectable distance and not climbed upon. Furthermore, it is inevitable that there are still traces of lead in various places and lead is a cumulative poison.

NOTE ON PRICES QUOTED IN THE TEXT

A question frequently asked is 'What would that sum be in today's money?'. Unfortunately, the answer is not a simple one. Take the example of £100, which would have been a reasonable annual income in the year 1807, when lead was discovered at Ballycorus. If you use the retail price index, this will translate into £7,565 in today's terms, or € 8,636 (taking 0.88 pounds to the Euro, which is a problem in itself); this would not be a good income today. If you use the labour value—which is the multiple of a worker's income that would be required to purchase the same goods—the figure would be £88,750 in today's money, or € 101,317. If you were to use relative income, which is a proportion of the GDP per head of population, the figure would be £98,030, or € 111,911. The final choice is the relative output—the amount of someone's income in comparison to the total output of the economy—by which the figure becomes £512,000 or € 584,500. If you are still following this, you can probably see why I don't tend to give modern equivalents of money from historical times, preferring the rather vague response that £100 in 1807 was a reasonable annual income.

GLOSSARY

As mining is a technical undertaking, there are certain terms used in this volume that may not be familiar to the reader. The glossary below seeks to explain these terms, though many of them are clarified in the main text. Other terms that may be similarly alien to the non-specialist reader are also included.

Adit A horizontal tunnel either leading into a mine or following a *lode*.

Antimony A substance used in metallic alloys such as that which makes up printers' type.

Blast engine An engine that forces air into a furnace to assist *smelting*.

Blast furnace A furnace for smelting ore by pumping compressed air into the furnace.

Buddle A shallow depression in the ground used in the process of separating the heavier lead from the lighter stone through the action of running water, with a rotating arm agitating the sediments to speed the process up.

Cantilevering A method of construction of projecting elements such as stairs that depends on the weight of a wall or other material to hold the projection in place. At Ballycorus the weight of the masonry in the chimney would have held the projecting stairs in place so that they appear to have no means of support at the outer end.

Cobbing Breaking up stone to separate the lead ore from the rock.

Crushing mill A mill used for crushing ore as an initial stage in sorting the ore from the *gangue*.

Dressed ore Ore that has been fully separated from the parent rock or *gangue* and which is ready for smelting.

Dressing The final stage in the separation of the ore from the *gangue*.

Dressing floor A paved surface, usually cobbled, used for spreading ore and on which labourers would separate the ore from the *gangue*. Also called a *picking floor* or a *knocking floor*.

Galena Lead sulphide; the principal mineral from which lead is obtained.

Gangue The unprofitable portion of the rock in which ore is found.

Grand jury The precursor of the county councils, in operation from the seventeenth century until 1898. They were bodies made up from among the principal landowners of the county other than peers. Among their responsibilities were the striking of the rate and the construction, repair and maintenance of roads and bridges.

Granite A hard, crystalline rock that occurs in many areas, including the area of the Dublin and Wicklow mountains stretching from Blackrock, Co. Dublin, to the north of County Wexford and the eastern part of Carlow. A variety of granite known as *pegmatite* occurs close to the edge of the granite mass and is rich in various minerals, particularly lead.

Knocking floor Another name for a *picking floor* or a *dressing floor*.

Level The portion of a mine in which a particular *lode* is exploited.

Litharge An oxide of lead, particularly that resulting from the refining of silver from lead.

Lode A vein of ore.

Mica schist A rock that is frequently found close to the granite. It is highly laminated, splitting easily along planes which are particularly shiny as a result of thin films of the mineral mica.

Native silver Silver metal found in the natural state, as opposed to silver oxide. It normally has a brown coloration on the surface.

Ore A naturally occurring mineral from which a more valuable substance may be recovered.

Pegmatite A form of granite that occurs in veins in the main granite mass. As a result of its being formed later than most of the rest of the granite, it contains minerals left over from the formation of the earlier rock. Amongst these is *galena*.

Picking floor An area paved with cobbles on which workers break up the produce of the mine to separate the ore from its matrix to as great a degree as possible.

Pig lead Ingots of refined lead.

Red lead An oxide of lead consisting of three atoms of lead and four of oxygen. Used in the manufacture of an anti-corrosion paint.

Refining furnace A furnace used to refine the metal from its impurities.

Reverberating furnace A furnace used in *smelting* wherein the flame turns back over the ore being heated.

Riddle house A building within a shot works where the manufactured shot is separated by means of a series of riddles into grades of different diameter.

Royalty A right granted to a miner or mining company to exploit land by mining it, subject to the payment of a percentage or fee to the landowner or the state.

Shaft A vertical cutting leading down to a *level* within a mine.

Sheet lead A flat form of lead metal usually manufactured by rolling but sometimes by casting. Used in roofing and in the past for lining coffins, water-tanks etc.

Shot tower A tower used for the manufacture of lead shot for guns, weights etc.

Slag hearth   A furnace, or hearth, for extracting lead from slags or poor ore.

Slime pit   A sedimentation tank used for settling the heavier galena out of a water-borne mixture of finely ground ore and matrix.

Smelting   Part of the process of removing the metal from its ore by applying heat, sometimes in the presence of a substance that will remove the unwanted part of the ore. Sulphur is removed from galena, or lead sulphide, through heating in the presence of oxygen, followed by further treatment to remove the oxygen.

Stampers   Machine-driven hammers used to break up the ore to assist in the separation of the *ore* from the *gangue*.

Stamping mill   Mill in which the ore and the rock to which it is attached are broken up by means of stampers.

Water-wheel   A mill-wheel. It used the action of water—either through its weight or its flow—to turn the wheel; the axle of the wheel then transmitted power to the machinery.

White lead   Lead carbonate. A white powder used in the manufacture of paint, though less so now than in the past.

Voussoir   Cut stone used to form an arch or vault.

1

LEAD

Lead is a soft, grey metal that has been known and used for thousands of years. It is too soft to be used for tools and weapons in the way that bronze and iron were, and it is not sufficiently attractive for decorative use, as are gold, silver and bronze. Nevertheless, lead has other properties that make it extremely useful for more mundane purposes. It is comparatively simple to recover from the ore, has a low melting-point and is fairly resistant to corrosion, so that it can be easily and cheaply produced for roofing, pipes and many other uses.

Pl. 1—Galena (lead sulphide).

It is most commonly found as lead sulphide, known as *galena*. This is a crystalline substance that looks very like metallic lead but has a distinctly cubic form (Pl. 1). It can be seen in rocks in the vicinity of the lead mines in Wicklow and Ballycorus. The process of removing the lead from the ore will be described in a later section, as it is important to the understanding of the remains of the lead works that can be seen today.

The melting-point of lead is only 328°C, as compared to gold (1,063°C), silver (962°C) and copper (1,083°C). Iron melts at the much higher temperature of 1,536°C and the technology to produce this heat was not developed until the fourteenth century. The low melting-point of lead allowed it to be used for low-technology purposes such as the casting of toys and, in the form of an alloy, as solder.

Over the centuries the greatest use of the metal has been in the form of sheet lead and lead pipes. Its soft but reasonably strong nature allows it to be hammered, rolled or drawn into various shapes. Sheet lead has been used extensively in roofing, either as a roof covering in its own right or as a supplement to slate to create waterproof joins with walls, chimneys etc. This is still an important use of the metal. Less common now is its use for guttering, hoppers and downpipes and the valleys of roofs, but these were very important uses until the early years of the twentieth century, and it still serves these purposes in historic buildings. Sheet lead was also used in the past for lining water-tanks and even coffins.

Lead pipes were extremely common in the past and this use reached its peak in the middle to late nineteenth century, when many municipal water schemes were established. The use of the water-closet increased demand for water-supply to homes, while the improvement in hygiene encouraged the installation of baths

Pl. 2—Roman lead pipe at Pompeii.

and wash-basins. The word *plumbing* comes from the Latin *plumbum*, meaning 'lead'. A plumber was originally someone who worked with lead, including roofing, but because of the large amount of pipework carried out by this trade the meaning of the word changed. The use of lead for water-pipes went out of favour in the twentieth century when copper pipes became more readily available, and later various plastics. The use of lead pipes was shown to result in tiny quantities of lead being dissolved in the water and this was harmful to health. In fact, it is said that an occupational disease of innkeepers was proved to be lead poisoning resulting from the consumption of the beer drawn at the start of the day, which had been sitting overnight in lead pipes. Many people today still run the water for a while before filling a kettle or a glass without knowing why they do it; it was the recommended practice in days gone by when water-pipes in houses were made of lead, whereas the water in the mains in the street was in iron pipes. It is strange that the research proving the harmful potential of lead water-pipes was carried out just *before* so many municipal water schemes were constructed, in Dublin and elsewhere, and yet this did not prevent its use. As with so many such issues, the arguments were not based on whether or not lead was harmful or whether it was present in the water carried in the pipes, but on what was a safe and acceptable level of contamination.

While lead was useless for weapons such as swords, arrowheads and spears, it came into its own with the development of small firearms, as it was a reasonably cheap metal that could easily be cast as bullets and recast by the soldiers. It is also easy to form into small spheres for use as gunshot and this process will also be described later, as shot-making was undertaken at Ballycorus.

Non-metallic lead has also been important, and the two principal forms are *red lead* and *white lead*. Red lead is an oxide of the metal and has been used in paints as a primer for rust pro-

Pl. 3—Lead water-tank, used as a flower tub.

tection. This use would have become progressively more important during the nineteenth century, as iron and steel were increasingly used for engineering projects such as ships and bridges. White lead is a carbonate of lead and has been used as a pigment in paint for a considerable period. In recent years its use has diminished, as the dangers of lead poisoning from paint have become better understood, but it is still used in certain paints, particularly for exterior use. Lead was also used in pottery glazes.

In the twentieth century certain uses of lead increased dramatically, such as for radiation shielding in radiology and in nuclear reactors, as an additive to petrol and in the plates of batteries, particularly those used in cars. These uses will not especially concern us here, however, as the lead works at Ballycorus and in Wicklow had disappeared before they became particularly significant.

2

LEAD IN THE DUBLIN AREA

Lead must have been mined in the Dublin area for centuries, and in the eighteenth century lead mines abounded all around the city. Transport was costly, particularly for bulky and heavy materials for building purposes, and so, as the built-up area of Dublin began to expand rapidly in the early eighteenth century, there grew up a search for local sources. Stone was available all around the city, as were sand and gravel. Lime could be produced from the local limestone, and bricks were fired from clays found as near as Merrion, Dolphin's Barn and the Moore Street area.

The sources of lead for roofing, gutters and pipes were also surprisingly close to the city. By the 1770s Dr John Rutty, in his *Natural History of the County of Dublin*, reported the existence of quite a number of lead mines and other sources of lead as yet untapped.[1] One mine was just at the southern edge of the Liberties, between New Street and New Row, probably close to where the South Circular Road now runs. At a quarry near St Stephen's Green another source of lead ore was discovered, and this seems to have been on the north side of Lower Baggot Street, close to the junction with Fitzwilliam Street. The smelting of lead took place at Dolphin's Barn at another quarry where lead had been discovered.

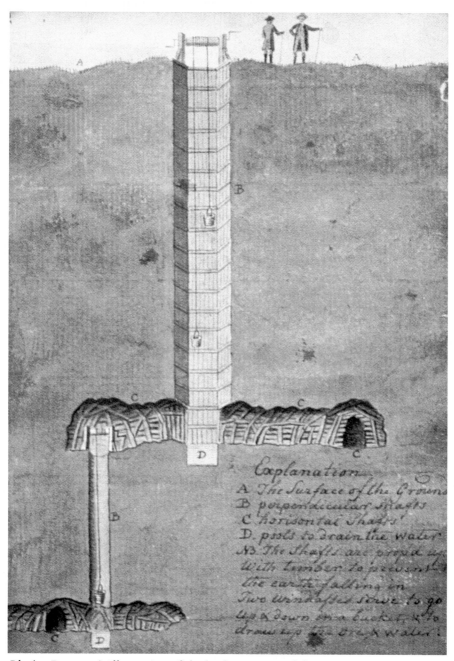

Pl. 4—Beranger's illustration of the lead mine at Dolphin's Barn (Royal Irish Academy).

A little further out from the city were still more lead mines. At Castleknock a mine was opened in the 1740s, and not far to the north of this, at Hunt's Town, a lead vein was discovered in the eighteenth century that was reported to seem promising. Further west again, at St Catherine's, near Lucan, a lead vein was worked for a while in this period. A quarry at Kilmainham was found to contain three veins of lead which were worked in the late 1760s, and between 60 and 70 tons were raised from this quarry in eighteen months. This high rate of production was further enhanced by a high content of silver, producing some 24 ounces of silver per ton. As we shall see, the Mining Company of Ireland was later to acquire a lead mine at Kilmainham. Lead deposits were also discovered in places as diverse as Dubber, Dunsink, Robswalls and Cloghran, and some of these districts produced more than one lead working.[2]

Perhaps the most curious of all these lead mines was at Clontarf. This vein was discovered near the shoreline and is reported to have been in use on and off since the time of King James I in the early seventeenth century. It was liable to be flooded by the tide; Rutty reported that in his time it was flooded with each incoming tide and had to be pumped and bailed out again before work could resume. As a result, it could only be worked for two to three hours out of each tide. This vein produced a rich ore, and it must have been productive to have made it worthwhile to go to so much trouble for so few hours' work. This mine was in use in the 1760s according to Rutty and was marked on Taylor's map of Dublin in 1816.[3] Lead was also found near Crab Lake in Clontarf, now the site of Kincora Court, though it was not deemed economic to exploit it.

The first-edition Ordnance Survey map of the Dublin area, published in 1843, marks a small circle on the strand just to the east of Castle Avenue, Clontarf, and opposite a quarry; the circle is labelled 'Hole made in search of Lead'. This is unlikely to be the shaft referred

to by Rutty and is more likely to be an early nineteenth-century ex-
cavation. Richard Griffith noted in 1828 that the lead vein 'at Clontarf is comparatively of recent discovery, and has been worked and
abandoned several times since February 1809, when the first shaft
was sunk'.[4] In 1822 it was reported that this mine was producing
metal worth up to £200 a week and this lead was being manufactured
into sheet lead and pipes at a mill in Palmerstown.[5] Griffith noted in
1828 that the first shaft, the only one of importance, was sunk to a
depth of 16yds (about 14.5m) and that a considerable body of ore
was raised in the last working of the mine, but the sides of the shaft
collapsed and the works were discontinued. Despite this comment
from an expert in mining geology, the mine was stated to be valuable
and producing the best quality of ore in the following year, when it
was sold to an unnamed Englishman with great practical experience
in mining; it was hoped that his example would result in a greater
amount of English capital being invested in Irish mining.[6] The Ordnance Survey 1:2,500-scale map of the area that was published in
1869 shows a second small circle on the shore and the two circles are
labelled 'Shafts made in search of Lead'. Lead was encountered on
the shore again in 1908 during works to provide main drainage,
which 'showed that the lead ore was by no means worked out'.[7]

Colm Lennon cites F.W.R. Knowles, author of *Old Clontarf*, as
stating that an abandoned shaft remained on the seafront in the early
twentieth century, while another stood on the foreshore, topped by
walls about 20ft thick. When the promenade was being developed
in the 1950s the shaft was filled in; the tower was cut down to sea-
wall height and made into the base of a circular shelter beside Clontarf baths.[8] The thickness of the walls seems to be a misinterpretation,
as the shelter is about 20ft, or 6m, across. The circular shape of this
shelter is precisely on the same spot as a circle of the same size shown
on the Ordnance Survey's 1:2,500 map of 1869 mentioned above;

Pl. 5—Former lead mine at Clontarf.

this circle is also on the map published in 1907, just before the sewer was laid along the seafront, lending credence to the proposition that this is the top of the mine shaft. The tower would have helped to exclude the tide from the mine shaft, making it easier to work the lead vein. The circular base of the shelter is constructed of local calp limestone, though heavily repaired with mass concrete.[9]

All of the lead deposits mentioned so far were in areas where the bedrock was limestone, and the lead veins would have run through that rock. Rutty also mentions discoveries of lead at Howth, where the principal rock is quartzite, though the lead was probably mined at the limestone quarries along the coast at Burrow Road.

For our purposes, however, lead that was found in the granite regions is particularly important. To the south-east of the city at Blackrock the limestone gives way to granite, and here at the boundary between the two rocks a lead vein was discovered in the late eighteenth century. This was found by a miner around about 1770 under the garden of Lady Arabella Denny at Lios an Uisce, opposite the end of Mount Merrion Avenue.[10] It is unlikely that this deposit was ever exploited, given its location in the garden of a member of the gentry.

Other lead veins in the granite region *were* mined. Two of these were at Dalkey and Killiney and had their heyday in the 1750s. A mining lease was granted to a partnership of individuals in 1749 in relation to lands at Mount Mapas.[11] This was the name by which Killiney Hill was known from the 1740s, after John Mapas, who lived at Rochestown House and who built the house later known as Killiney Castle (now Fitzpatrick's Hotel). He also surrounded the hill

Pl. 6—Detail of Rocque's map of 1760, showing lead mines at Sorrento, Dalkey.

with a stone wall. By 1753 'a vein of great thickness' had been discovered on the lands and the mines were reported to be flourishing.[12] In 1750 the same group of individuals took a mining lease of land in Dalkey, and they worked both mines for a few years.[13] There were various changes in the partnership over time, and some differences between the mining rights at the two sites and in the ownership of the mines. At Killiney John Mapas made sure that the lease included a clause allowing his son to share in the value of the ore. He was entitled to one sixth of the produce of the mine provided that he paid one sixth of the cost.

By 1757 the mine at Dalkey had come into the possession of the Mines Royal Minerals Mineral and Battery Works of London but it did not last long under this ownership either.[14] It was worked again around 1780 but, as before, it was short-lived. The mines were shown on John Rocque's map of County Dublin, published in 1760, which shows that they were close to the shore where Sorrento Terrace now stands.[15] They appear again on the later maps of Taylor and Skinner (1783) and John Taylor (1816) and were later acquired by the Mining Company of Ireland.[16] Some traces of these mines still remain in the grounds of houses along the northern shore of Killiney Bay at Sorrento Road.

Those who know the coast at Killiney Bay would be more familiar with the lead mine at Killiney, as this had part of its working at White Rock, below Vico Road. Here is a cave at the base of the granite cliffs, known as Decco's Cave. This is not a natural cave but is the adit, or near-horizontal tunnel, to a lead mine which penetrated the cliff at this point. Rutty reported that this mine at Killiney produced a rich ore that contained considerable quantities of silver.[17] Like its counterpart at Dalkey, this mine did not last long and a later attempt to work it in the 1780s was also unsuccessful.[18] In the 1820s two veins of lead were mined on the eastern slopes of these hills by the Royal Irish Mining Company; a significant amount of lead ore was raised from a number of shallow shafts, though the lead veins were found to be irregular and unproductive and were abandoned.[19]

Associated with these mines was a lead-smelting works on Dalkey Common, run by the same partnership that worked the mines. The

Pl. 7—Decco's Cave, former lead mine at White Rock, Killiney.

smelting works stood where the road runs to the front of Sorrento Terrace, close to the corner at the gates to Sorrento Park. One of the castles in Dalkey village, leased from Thomas Archbold, was used to store the lead.[20]

Francis Elrington Ball in his *History of the County Dublin* mentions a lead mine at Rochestown near Dalkey, with a smelting house on Dalkey Common.[21] The lands of Rochestown, centred on Rochestown House, which stood close to where the modern Killiney Shopping Centre now stands, extended over a wide area from Sallynoggin to the coast. The reference to mines at Rochestown relates to the mine at Mount Mapas, with its adit at White Rock and a shaft higher up the hill.

The mines at Killiney and Dalkey lay near the edge of the granite. Here the hard, crystalline granite gives way to the greenish-grey, highly laminated mica schist, which is created from sedimentary rocks by the intense heat of the granite when it was formed deep

underground some 600 million years ago. Just as the schist was baked
by the granite, the granite was cooled near the edge by the influence
of the surrounding rock and as a result it differs somewhat from the
form which is found deeper in the granite mass. Sometime after it
was intruded into the underlying rock, fissures opened up in the
granite; minerals such as galena and sphalerite entered the fissures,
forming veins, mainly in the granite but also extending into the mica
schist.[22] These veins vary in thickness and also in the concentration
of galena in the surrounding stone, and so some deposits are easier
to work than others and their profitability varies.

Another variant in the quality of the lead is the content of silver,
as this lead ore usually contains a certain amount of the more valuable
metal. The quantities are quite small, typically being about 140g per
tonne of the ore, equivalent to one part in more than seven
thousand.[23] The amount of silver is important for two reasons. First,
it is only economic to extract it if there is more than a certain quantity
present, and in the eighteenth century this proportion was high. No
less than thirteen ounces of silver per ton (360g per tonne) would be
necessary for economic extraction, as some ten to fifteen per cent of
the lead would be lost in the separation process, which required a
great deal of coal to heat the lead. As we will see, this situation improved in the nineteenth century as technology progressed. Second,
the presence of silver in sheet lead made it more brittle. As the use of
lead for roofing and gutters depended on working it into shape,
brittle lead was inferior as it may develop hairline cracks, resulting
in leaks.

Given the geology of the Dalkey and Killiney mines, it is surprising that other parts of the granite close to the junction with the mica
schist were not explored in the 1750s when these mines opened.
Another place where there is a significant boundary between the two
rocks is the hillside between Shankill and Kilternan, the area known

as Ballycorus; curiously, it was not until early in the nineteenth century that lead was discovered here. At that time searches were carried out along the entire junction between the granite and the mica schist and as a result lead veins were worked along that line at Dalkey, Killiney, Ballycorus, Powerscourt, Djouce, Lough Bray, Lough Dan, Glendasan, Glendalough, Glenmalure and Shillelagh.[24] Many of these proved not to be productive and the only ones to show any degree of success were at Ballycorus, Glendasan, Glendalough and Glenmalure.

As the boundaries between land ownerships or townlands do not necessarily respect geological boundaries, it is not surprising that the discovery of lead at Ballycorus resulted in similar exploration in the adjoining townland of Rathmichael. The landlords of Rathmichael and Shankill were the Domvile family, but while the Domviles had a long lease from the 1690s they were not the owners of the head lease. Their lease was from the archbishop of Dublin and did not include the mining rights. In September 1807 the archbishop granted a lease of the mining rights to John Blacker in exchange for one eighth of the produce of any mines.[25] This agreement included the archbishop's entire Shankill estate with both Shankill and Rathmichael townlands, extending to 946 plantation acres or more than 1,500 statute acres, or 620 hectares, coinciding with the land leased to the Domviles. Most of this land, however, was geologically unlikely to produce any lead mines. In the following year Blacker sold a quarter share in the mines to Alderman Nathaniel Hone, presumably to raise capital to develop the mines. This Nathaniel Hone was not either of the well-known artists of this name, Nathaniel Hone the elder having died before this time, while Nathaniel Hone the younger had not yet been born.[26] The name Nathaniel has been used over many generations in the Hone family and no doubt he was related to both painters.

Pl. 8—Former lead mine at Sorrento, Dalkey.

The lead-mining enterprise was carried on at Shankill for about ten years, though it is not known what quantity of lead was raised from these mines. By 1818 the mines at Rathmichael had failed and John Blacker was declared bankrupt.[27] He surrendered his mining lease to the archbishop and five years later the rights were again leased, this time to a chemist from Capel Street in Dublin named Andrew Redmond.[28] He mortgaged the property three years later and little is heard of the mines again after this. It seems likely that they failed, as they are not mentioned in the various surveys of the district that were carried out in the 1830s. A number of mine shafts are shown in Rathmichael townland on the first-edition Ordnance Survey map, as we shall see later, and one single shaft was shown in Shankill townland, very close to the boundary with Ballycorus and Rathmichael.

3

THE EARLY DAYS AT BALLYCORUS

Ballycorus is the area between Shankill and Kilternan, Co. Dublin, which stretches from the chimney at the top of the hill westwards and north-westwards down the slope to the valley bottom. The eastern and north-eastern slopes of the hill are in Rathmichael townland, while the northern slope and the hill to the south of Ballycorus and Rathmichael are in the townland of Shankill. The hill itself is a low ridge which has its highest point southwards from Ballycorus at Carrickgollagan, better known locally as Katty Gollagher or Katty Gallagher. The Ballycorus chimney is on the crest towards the northern end of the ridge.

At the beginning of the nineteenth century Ballycorus was a farming area with a great variety of land quality. The upper slopes of the hill were rough heath or gorse, much as they are now, but without the Scots pines or the more densely planted trees. At the bottom of the valley there was a bog which was not much used except for game shooting; it was reclaimed through drainage in the 1840s.[1] Between the heath and the bog there was farmland, and the inhabitants of the townland of Ballycorus would have been mainly farmers and farm labourers until the discovery of lead. Even then the use of most of the land at Ballycorus continued to be agricultural.

Pl. 9—Boundary between granite (left) and mica schist (right) at Ballycorus.

Lead was first discovered in Ballycorus in about 1806; by the following January some mining was being carried out, and the indications were that it would be very productive. The ore was found to be very pure, producing 80% lead by weight.[2] The lead had a high content of silver but it was not considered worthwhile to remove it, as the price of lead was high without going to the trouble of processing it to remove the silver, particularly as some lead would have been lost in the process. In July 1807 a 31-year lease was granted to a Cornish man, Thomas Prout, permitting him to discover and mine lead at Ballycorus and the adjoining lands of Johnstown to the west.[3] His rent for this lease was to be one eighth of the profits of the mine except in the first year, when it would be only a one-ninth share. At the same time, Prout entered into partnership with Eliza and Mary Anne Mowlds, who had agreed to put up an eighth of the cost of working the mine in exchange for an equivalent share.[4] Three months later, in October 1807, Thomas Prout sold a further quarter share in the mine to Alderman Nathaniel Hone for £1,000, and this arrangement included the grant of exclusive rights to Hone to act as agent for the produce of the mines.[5] It seems probable that this fairly substantial sum of money was to be used to pay for the cost of developing the mine, not only through digging for ore but also in the erection of buildings to service the workings. This was the same Nathaniel Hone who was to take on a quarter share in the mines on the adjoining Rathmichael and Shankill lands in the following year, as we have seen. The mines got under way and were given the name Mount Peru, somewhat pretentiously—even optimistically—given that Peru was a country with great mineral wealth. In August 1808 a further four shares in the mine were advertised for sale, again presumably to raise capital to continue to improve the mines. The mine was described as a 'truly valuable concern'—'the quality of the ore (being the richest in the United Kingdom,) and the daily improving condition of the Mine, are too well known to render any recommendation necessary'.[6] The initial mine workings were augmented in the following year, when a second vein of lead was discovered.[7]

In this initial phase of mining at Ballycorus the mines were opencast, whereby the miners excavate into the surface of the ground rather than sinking shafts into the rock below. Initially the workings extended over a length of about 40m and were dug about 2m into the rock. The mineral that was being mined was lead sulphide, or galena, which was found to occur in veins that were generally little more than 0.5m wide. For the most part the galena was in small grains, though some larger crystals were found, and the lead ore was mixed with a variety of other minerals, including lead carbonate, antimony and pyrites.[8]

Pl. 10—Site of opencast mining at Ballycorus.

In 1814 Eliza and Mary Anne Mowlds decided to dispose of their share in the mines and at this stage there were nine other partners in the enterprise, including Thomas Prout and Nathaniel Hone. Of the other partners the most significant was George Casson, who by this time had a significant interest in the land of Ballycorus. In the following year he acquired the leasehold interest in the land and shortly afterwards became the sole owner of the mine.[9] It would seem that at this time the value of the mine was not realising the original expectations—or, to put it another way, the cost of raising the ore was a greater part of the value than anticipated— as Casson's lease required him to pay only one third of the previous rent, being one 24th of the value of the lead raised rather than the previous one eighth. By 1818 Casson was advertising the lease of the mines and he was prepared to consider the formation of a com-

pany for the purpose of extending the works, 'of which it is emi-
nently capable'.[10] This is a strong indication that the mines were
struggling through lack of capital to exploit them fully rather than
the lack of promise of further profitability, given adequate investment.

As a mark of his strong belief in the future of the mine, in the
same advertisement Casson sought proposals for the building of a
smelting house on the premises. By March 1819 the smelting works
had been erected and Casson was advertising the sale of pig lead—
lead cast into bars, which could then be melted again to be formed
into pipes or sheet lead or for other purposes.[11] He failed, however,
to attract any potential buyer for the lease or investors to set up a
company; by April 1820 he was bankrupt and the property was advertised for auction.[12] The notice of the auction stated that Casson
had expended considerable sums of money in buildings associated
with the mine and workmen's houses in addition to the smelting
works, and offered the opinion that 'these concerns, if judiciously
worked, would produce immense profit to any company or indi-
vidual, who would advance a capital of from £3 to £5,000'. The
ore raised from the mine was said to be of excellent quality and to
be worth £8 to £15 per ton.

George Casson's lease of the land at Ballycorus and the mining
rights were sold in November 1820 to Thomas Thompson for a
mere £100, and this also suggests that the mines were thought to
be of little value or would only be of value if significant sums were
invested in them.[13] Thompson planted trees on the land for their
timber value, and it seems likely that these were the Scots pines
that still stand on the land today. In the following March he sublet
the land and its mines to Cheyne Brady and Henry Hodgson for
an initial payment of £100, which ensured that he cleared his own
costs while retaining his rights to the timber.[14] Brady and Hodgson

Pl. 11—Scots pines at Ballycorus.

were required to keep the mine working; if they still had it at the end of a year, they were to pay Thompson a further £400. This was in addition to the one-24th share of the ore that they would have to pay, and so Thompson stood to gain a handsome 400% profit on his outlay if the mine continued to be worked despite having no risk, as he had already regained his £100 outlay. Cheyne Brady and Henry Hodgson were cousins and they became well known for their mining exploits, moving on from Ballycorus to Glendalough, where they acquired another lead mine, as discussed below, and to Avoca, where they controlled extensive copper mines at Ballymurtagh. Hodgson was a founder of the Wicklow Copper Mining Company and went on to own mines in County Galway.[15]

5

THE MINING COMPANY'S ACQUISITION OF BALLYCORUS

Amongst the first endeavours of the Mining Company of Ireland was the acquisition of the lead workings at Ballycorus. By 1825 the mine at Ballycorus was in the hands of Richard Samuel Brady, probably a relative of Cheyne Brady—perhaps his son, brother or other close relative, as he had taken on the administration of the estate of Cheyne Brady, who had died intestate a year or so previously.[1] Richard Brady also had a corn mill a little downstream from the Ballycorus lead works at Ticknick.[2] In February 1825 he leased most of his interest in the mining at Ballycorus to the Mining Company through its secretary, Robert Purdy.[3] Two plots of land were excluded from this lease. Brady had started to build a shot tower on the property, and he retained the rights to a plot of land twenty yards square on which this tower would stand, together with the necessary rights of access to it. He also retained the smelting works lower down the hillside, below the mines. The rent to be paid to Brady was £30 a year plus the one-24th share in the ore which still needed to be paid to the ground landlord. Later in the year Brady granted a lease on an additional area of land to the company.[4] He died in 1827.[5]

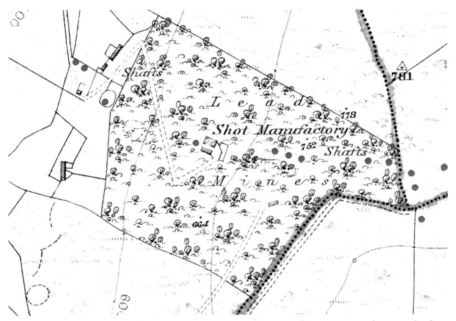

Pl. 12 —The 1843 Ordnance Survey map, showing shot tower and mine shafts. Three shafts are seen at Rathmichael at right, with one at Shankill below.

SHOT TOWER

The shot tower that Brady built on the land was fairly high up the hill slope on the site of the original mine shaft. For reasons that will become apparent, this site was at quite a remove from the main lead works at the foot of the hill.

Lead shot is comprised of small spheres of lead and is used in shotgun cartridges and as weights for various purposes, such as fishing lines. While larger spheres, such as those used in muskets, could be formed in moulds, it would be difficult and impractical to do this in the large quantities and small size required for shot. Instead, it is formed in shot towers. This process uses a property of liquids whereby they will form into spherical droplets if allowed to fall through the air. Usually this can be achieved by using an old vertical

Pl. 13—Site of Richard Brady's shot tower at Ballycorus.

mine shaft, though in the absence of sufficient height a tower would be built over the shaft. Molten lead is hoisted to the top and poured into a colander to help it to break up into droplets, and as it falls it will separate into small spheres. Provided that the shaft is high enough, the falling lead will cool sufficiently to solidify before it reaches the bottom, where it falls into a water bath, both to cushion its fall to ensure that the drops remain spherical and to complete the cooling process.

Brady's shot tower was high, presumably constructed of stone, and had a wooden section at the top.[6] It was marked on the first-edition Ordnance Survey map of this area, published in 1843. This shows the tower to have been on a site significantly above any other buildings of the time, but all that is visible now is a small platform artificially cut into the hillside to provide a base for the shot works. The location of the tower would have been determined by the pres-

ence of a suitable disused mine shaft, and coal would have had to
be carried up here to provide the heat for melting the lead.

BALLYCORUS ROAD

From the outset, lead ore, coal and finished lead needed to be
moved from place to place. As Ballycorus was not near a large river,
a canal or the sea, the only method of transport was by road. It
seems likely, then, that Ballycorus Road, leading from Kilternan to
connect with the existing roads at Cherrywood on the way to
Loughlinstown, was built partly in order to provide a decent access
to the Ballycorus lead mines. The road does not appear on John
Rocque's map of County Dublin, published in 1760, but is marked
as a 'New Road' on John Taylor's map of 1816.[7] A little earlier than
this it appears as 'New Road' on a manuscript map of part of the
Domvile estate at Rathmichael dated 1812.[8] The road would also
have served to connect the district to the new mail-coach road
through Loughlinstown and Bray. This was a period of great road-
building, but there can be no doubt that the lead works would have
had a strong influence on the construction of this road. There is a
possibility that packhorses or mules were used initially for the transportation to Ballycorus, though wheeled transport was certainly in
use by the 1840s, when Robert Kane wrote that 'the dressed ore is
brought on cars to the company's smelting works at Ballycorus'.[9]

6

THE MINING COMPANY'S FORTUNES

The Mining Company of Ireland was employing some 1,400 workers by the end of 1826, less than three years after its formation.[1] In its first full year, 1825, it had raised £6,400 worth of minerals. This increased to £14,200 in 1826 and to £21,500 in 1827. Things certainly looked promising and the reports of mining experts on the quality of ore in the mines were encouraging.[2]

Just as the young company got going, however, external factors came into play which very nearly destroyed it. In the mid-1820s the economy went into a major slump. As is usual in depressions, the construction industry was badly hit and the price of lead and copper plummeted. Lead was particularly badly hit, and the initial price of £27 or even £30 a ton which the company had received for its ore dropped rapidly to £16.[3] Moreover, an act of parliament passed in 1825 permitted the importation of foreign lead ore at a greatly reduced level of duty, thus increasing competition for the reduced levels of sales on the home market.[4] As a result, the company's lead mines were severely hit and only those that could produce ore very cheaply survived. By 1827 only the Luganure mines at Glendalough and those at Kildrum in Donegal were still in operation.[5] Some of the initial mines, such as Kilmainham and

Dalkey, seem never to have been exploited by the Mining Company, while the land leased at Ticknick failed to produce any sign of lead at all. The fate of the Ballycorus mines will be discussed later, but suffice it to say that they did not produce lead at a low enough price to make it worthwhile working them during the depression.

The mines at Kildrum, Co. Donegal, proved to be very profitable initially, producing some 60 tons of lead ore per month, but this did not last—for technical reasons rather than any inadequacy in the ore. In 1828 there was a prolonged drought which, paradoxically, prevented the mine from being worked because of flooding. Most of the mines used water-power to run the pumps that kept the deep mines dry; during the drought there was insufficient water to run the machinery and the pumps could not operate. As work progressed on the mine, the amount of water seeping in increased, and the company had to purchase more machinery continually to keep pace. By 1831 the battle was clearly hopeless, and the flow of water was increasing faster than new equipment could be installed. The Kildrum mine was closed early in 1832, leaving only the Glendalough mines producing lead for the company.[6]

The price of lead and copper continued to fall into the 1830s, and even the Glendalough mines, which could produce lead at very cheap rates, became unprofitable. By 1832 the company had only five mines left in operation: one copper mine in County Waterford, the collieries at Slievardagh in Tipperary, slate mines at Killaloe and in County Waterford, and the lead workings in the Glendalough area. In addition to this there was the Ballycorus lead works, but this was also in financial difficulties owing to the very small amounts of lead which the company was mining. On top of all this, with losses almost across the board every year, the company found that it was owed £10,000 by Lord Audley, on whose lands lay one of the failed copper workings in west Cork, and the peer

Pl. 15—Mine buildings near the Hero mine, Glendasan.

to distinguish it from the original, which was known as the Luganure mine. In May 1827 lead was discovered at two other locations in the Glendasan valley, one of which showed promise of good productivity. The cost of producing dressed ore from these mines at this time was £1 5*s* at the Hero mine and £1 at Luganure, and although the price of lead was falling at this time the company could still get £9 a ton for the ore.[15] The opening of the Hero mine was well timed, as it came soon after production at the Luganure mine was suspended pending the completion of a new level through which the mine would be drained. As it happened, this mine was out of production for three or four years and the Hero mine provided the income for extensive exploration and improvement at the mines at this time. Extensive facilities for processing the material from the mines were provided near the Hero mine, including dressing floors.

The first-edition Ordnance Survey map of the area shows three lead mines at the Hero site, with a pump and a pumping wheel marked at a site downhill from two of the mines, to which they are connected by a dashed line labelled 'Range of Pumping Machine'.[16] This appears to be a flat rod system, whereby the water-wheel is located on a mill-race remote from the mine shaft and the power from the wheel is conveyed by a system of rods to the mine, allowing the mine to be drained even though it is not adjacent to the source of the power. The map also shows a mill for grinding ore, the ruins of which may still be seen at the site today.

The expansion and new exploration in the late 1820s came at a bad time, as the price of lead was falling dramatically. In addition, not all expenditure was to prove worthwhile—for example, the extensive work carried out in opening a new mine on Brockagh Mountain, which is on the northern side of the valley, opposite Camaderry on the southern side. Following considerable exploratory work, the cutting of a new adit here started in 1829 and carried on for two years. Finally, in April 1831, the shaft was broken through to reach the lode; it was immediately decided that this was not a profitable deposit and work was suspended.[17]

In the meantime, the decision of the grand jury, which was the authority responsible for roads before the establishment of the county councils, to construct a new road from Hollywood to Glendalough through the Wicklow Gap was seen by the company as having the potential to increase the value of the mine, as it would pass very close.[18] The cost of constructing a road such as this would usually be paid by the ratepayers of the county, but in this case the Commissioners for Encouraging Public Works paid a considerable part of the cost. Work on the Luganure mine was suspended pending the construction of this road in order to get as much value out of it as possible. This would have been an easy decision to take, as

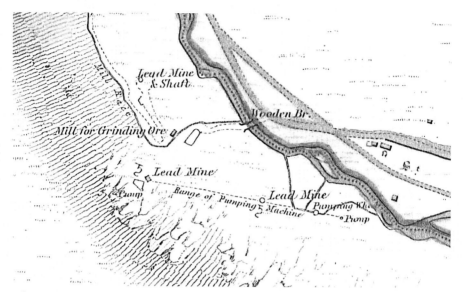

Pl. 16—Ordnance Survey map of 1838, showing the Hero mine, Glendasan (courtesy of Trinity College, Dublin).

the depressed state of the lead market meant that the mines were producing more lead than the company could sell. In fact, by 1830 the lead mines in the Glendalough area were making a loss.[19]

For the next few years the low price of lead left the mines in a very poor financial state, and they showed a loss every year from late 1830 to 1834. The loss was at its greatest in 1833 at nearly £1,800, and in 1834 it was £1,100. During this time various measures were adopted to minimise this loss, including the suspension of any improvement works when losses were particularly high, and the rates of pay for the workers were reduced towards the end of 1832.[20]

In 1835 the fortunes of the mine took a turn for the better. A small profit at the beginning of the year increased as time went on and the profit on the year was more than £450. The change in circumstances brought an increase in the rate of improvements at the mines; these included sixteen new houses for workers in that year, the opening of a new mine known as 'Ruplagh' and the improvement in the drainage of the Luganure mine.[21] This showed a belief in the potential of the district to return to profit, a faith that was proven in 1836 when the Glendalough mines returned a massive profit of almost £3,900, representing a profit in this single year which exceeded the entire loss over the four and a half years at the beginning of the decade.[22] The improved fortunes led to enhancements of the workings through the addition of a crushing mill for dressing ores, an additional dressing floor and new roads, along with four more houses for miners.

In 1837 the price of lead fell again, and the company had to curtail expenditure at Glendalough once more, though the profits were reasonably good in the early part of the year. This was repeated in 1838, when the mines returned high profits in the first half but barely scraped a profit in the second. This time the cause was partly due to the suspension of work in the Luganure mine while new ventilation shafts were cut. Works also included the erection of a new water-wheel to drive machinery for lifting the ore to the surface to replace the previous horse-powered arrangement. The interruption at Luganure continued into 1839, but the mine returned to profitability later and brought in a total profit of about £1,000 for the year.[23]

Throughout this period the price of lead fluctuated wildly, and the mines swung from profit to loss quite rapidly. This was the case again in 1840, when a large loss of more than £1,800 in the first half of the year was less than offset by a profit in the second half. In 1840 a new lode was discovered at the foot of Luganure Mountain at Glendasan, and by 1842 this was producing significant quantities of ore. This did not prevent the mines from becoming unprofitable again, however, as the early 1840s was a time of low lead prices. By 1844 the Ruplagh mine was losing money and the decision was taken to abandon the lower parts of the mine. The discovery of new lodes, to be known as 'North Ruplagh' and 'North Luganure', was a source of optimism, but even when the mines returned to profitability in the mid-1840s the profits remained extremely low.[24]

The Luganure vein was described at this time as being 1,645m long and 330m deep, normally being around 1.5m wide but expanding in one place to 3.6m in width.[25] It yielded between 0.5 and 0.75 tons of galena per cubic metre, about 70 per cent of which was lead. Another vein about a metre wide lay a little to the west.

In 1851 the Mining Company negotiated a new lease with the archbishop of Dublin and availed of new legislation which allowed for more favourable leases for mining. The archbishop was a willing and encouraging lessee and facilitated the new lease for forty-one years at the same rent as the previous lease.[26]

Throughout all the times of depression the company continued to improve its mines and to seek new lodes. In 1850, although prices were still poor and profitability low, a new stamping mill was installed for pulverising the poorer-quality ores with lower proportions of lead that had accumulated over the years because they had not been worth the labour of extracting the galena, or lead sulphide, by hand.[27] This was a great success in improving operations and the decision was taken almost immediately to enlarge it.[28] Other improvements at this time included the driving of a new shaft deep into Luganure Mountain—better known as Camaderry Mountain—in order to reopen the original Luganure mine, which had been abandoned some years before. This new shaft was under construction over a period of several years and it was intended that it would continue further down into the valley from the Wicklow Gap in order to provide a means of draining the mine of water. Eventually, after years of work, a shaft more than 80m deep was cut, but it was abandoned when calculations showed that it would be necessary to continue for 1,460m to achieve the objective, at a cost of £10,000; furthermore, it was concluded that 'the time occupied in its completion would have seen, perhaps, the whole of the then shareholders in their graves'.[29]

In the 1850s the mines at Glendalough returned to profit, and by the middle of the decade profits of £5,000 to £7,000 were being returned each year. This slowed down a little towards the end of the decade, but nevertheless annual profits remained around £4,000 to £5,000 into the 1860s.[30]

THE MINING COMPANY AT BALLYCORUS

As has been seen, one of the new Mining Company of Ireland's early acquisitions was the lead mine at Ballycorus, which was purchased as a going concern in February 1825.[1] Along with the mines themselves, the company acquired some twelve acres of land with several dwelling houses, a store, a smithy and a dressing house. In the latter building the lead ore was dressed to remove as much of the lead ore as possible from its parent rock, this being a basic part of the work carried out at a mine before the ore is sent for smelting. The houses were let to miners, providing a rental income for the company.

By the following July the mines were producing ore in considerable quantity at a reasonable cost. The company's mines in the Glendalough area had also produced significant amounts of lead and it was thought likely that lead would be raised locally at Dalkey and Ticknick—trials at Ticknick were carried on in the early months of the company's existence and appeared to be favourable.[2]

With this quantity of lead ore at its disposal, the company decided to acquire the lead works at Ballycorus in order to smelt its own lead and gain a further advantage on the market. It was reported that the Ballycorus lead works consisted at this time of ex-

Pl. 17—Miner at work in Wicklow, 1850s.

tensive buildings with a watercourse and pond, a reverberating furnace and a refining furnace, two slag hearths, a blast engine and
stampers, powered by a water-wheel. In all, some £3,000 was said
to have been spent on the works before they were acquired by the
company.[3]

The water that ran the wheel was obtained from a small river
which winds its way from the hillside above Kilternan to the sea at

Shanganagh. For its size and location this stream was quite indus-
trialised, with paper and cotton mills in operation at Kilternan, a
corn mill just downstream from Ballycorus at Ticknick and another
corn mill at Shanganagh.[4] Previously there had been other mills at
Mullinastill (as the name suggests) and at Loughlinstown. To service the water-wheel, the lead works had its own millpond at a distance upstream, and water was conducted along the side of the
slope to the large wheel in order to get sufficient height to run it.

The Mining Company of Ireland began smelting lead at the Ballycorus lead works on 4 August 1825 and it was expected that the
works would produce fifteen tons of lead per week.[5] Within six
months of the purchase of the works the company had processed
some 70 tons of lead there, with a value of £1,730; this was considered to be a favourable figure, as the cost of the works to the
company had been only £875.[6] It is tempting to think that the purchase of the lead works for only £875 when £3,000 had been spent
on their construction was due to the Mining Company's near-mon-
opoly of lead-mining in Ireland. If the company was not going to
supply lead ore to the works, then who would? Not so favourable
as the smelting works, however, was the mining side of the operations at Ballycorus. The Ballycorus mine did not live up to its initial expectations and operations were reduced.[7] On the adjoining
lands of Ticknick the company failed to find lead and this project
was abandoned. The Dalkey lead works also ceased to appear in
the company's records at this time and the Ballycorus lead works
was forced to rely mainly on the ore from the Glendalough area.

Early in 1826 matters improved, as the Ballycorus mine went
back into profit and some 54 tons of lead ore were brought from
the Kildrum mine in Donegal, presumably by sea, to be smelted at
Ballycorus.[8] The improvement was short-lived, however, as by the
end of 1826 the market for lead had slumped and the mine had

become unprofitable again. The lead works also suffered in the slump, as it became difficult to find buyers for the pig lead, or blocks of lead, produced. The company decided that, as the water-power available at the lead works was significantly greater than was necessary to run the smelting works, the works should be expanded to include a greater degree of manufacturing in order to improve the sales. The decision was taken, therefore, to divert a significant amount of the power from the water-wheel to machinery for rolling lead into sheets and for drawing it into pipes.[9]

Work went ahead on the expansion of the lead works in 1827, the same year that the decision was taken to abandon the Ballycorus mine for the time being. By mid-1828, a new 30ft-diameter water-wheel, 4ft wide, had been erected to serve the new processes, but the start of operations was delayed when a contractor failed to deliver the castings necessary for the rolling mill until the end of the year.[10] The Ballycorus lead works started to manufacture sheet lead and lead pipes early in 1829 and in the same year acquired the shot works with its shot tower and its machinery, its builder, Richard Brady, having died in 1827.[11]

The Ballycorus lead works was initially a great success. The company reported that respectable architects, plumbers and builders recommended its products, and the works helped to ensure that the produce of the lead mines found a market. In addition, experiments at Ballycorus showed that the company's mines produced lead that was well suited to the manufacture of white lead, the main pigment used in making white paint at that time. Unwilling to venture into further new products, the company decided to find a practical man of some capital who would make white lead under the auspices of the company; unfortunately, no one of that description came forward and no further attempt was made to produce white lead at this stage.[12]

While the Ballycorus works were successful in theory, they still depended on there being a market for lead. To some extent they helped the company to sell its lead, as manufactured lead was easier to sell than lead ingots or pig lead. As the price of lead continued to fall, however, the amount of lead being produced by the mines declined dramatically. The Kildrum lead mines in Donegal closed in 1832, leaving only the mines in the Glendalough area to supply the Ballycorus works, and in the same year the company also closed its Audley copper mine in west Cork and surrendered its agreement for a lease of a colliery at Tullynaha in Leitrim.[13] Ballycorus made a small loss in 1832, the demand for manufactured lead being reasonable but only at low prices.[14] There was a further small loss in 1833, when the amount of lead produced by the Glendalough mines was too small to keep the lead works fully employed.[15]

Matters began to improve in 1834 as the price of lead began to climb again. The lead works went back into profit and by the end of the year matters had improved so much that it was decided to reopen the Ballycorus lead mine. This entailed pumping the water out of it, but by early 1835 it was decided that the mine was not promising. Enough lead was recovered from the mine to cover most of the £40 or so spent on the investigation and then the mine was allowed to flood again.[16]

IMPROVEMENTS, 1835 AND ONWARDS

Just as the price of lead climbed again and the company looked forward to reasonable profits from this side of its operations, the Ballycorus lead works ran into technical difficulties. In 1835, during the course of normal operations, one of the rollers in the mill that produced sheet lead broke. As a result, the rolling mill was out of action for two months. This was a setback but not a disaster, as the

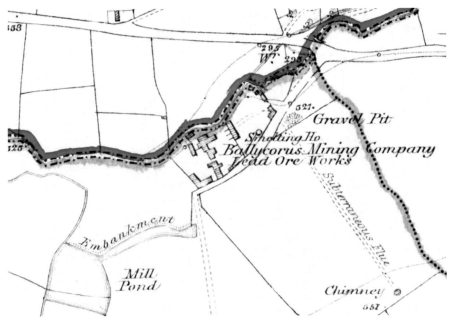

Pl. 18—Ordnance Survey map of 1843, showing Ballycorus lead works and chimney.

works managed to turn in a profit for the year despite the problems. Other improvements were also carried out, including the addition of new stables and the overhaul of the furnaces.[17]

In the following year major new works were carried out to take advantage of the now-prosperous state of the lead trade and the increase in the amount of lead being produced from the mines. A new smelting house was built, housing two furnaces. Along with this came a major new development—the construction of a new chimney. Up to then the works had a chimney to vent the furnaces, but this was causing problems. At that time industries tended to be located in valleys in order to avail of the water-power from the local stream. This was the case at Ballycorus, where there was a 30ft water-wheel to drive various parts of the machinery in the manufacturing process. Being low down in the valley, fumes from the chimney tended to remain locally rather than being dispersed into the atmosphere. This was bad enough with the smoke from steam engines, but in the case of a smelting works the fumes would contain poisonous lead. As a result, there were allegations that cattle were being poisoned in the locality. The answer would be to construct a new chimney at a higher elevation. Not only would it disperse the poisonous fumes further afield but also it would ensure that the fumes contained less lead, as the chimney was designed to solidify as much of the metal as possible before being vented into the atmosphere. For this purpose a smoke house was erected on the course of the flue to aid the condensation of lead and any other metals that were escaping in the smoke and polluting the area.[18]

The new chimney was built at a distance from the lead works up the hillside, some 50ft (15m) in vertical distance above the furnaces. An underground flue, 5ft high and 3½ft wide, brought the flue gases up to the chimney. At the upper end of this flue stood the chimney, which was 90ft high and 10ft in diameter at the base, tapering to 4½ft at the top.[19] There is some disagreement about the length of the flue. The mining company's half-yearly report in December 1836 states that it was 930ft long, while the Ordnance Survey's field name book gives a figure of 'about 200 yards', which would be only 600ft.[20] Measurement from the Ordnance Survey's first-edition six-inch map, published in 1843, gives a distance of 240m from the works to the chimney.[21] This is substantially different from the figure in the company's report, which translates as 283.5m. If, however, allowance is made for the distance between the smelter and the point where the flue crossed the boundary of the works, the 930ft, or 283.5m, appears to be correct. The point at which this flue left the works can still be seen, as there is a large arch in the boundary wall, now stopped up with concrete blocks, not far from the gateway. This arch is below the level of the adjacent road, as the flue would have passed beneath the road.

The cost of the chimney and its flue was considerable, amounting to over £1,200, and the new furnaces and other improvements cost a further £300. The lead trade had improved so much by this time that, although the new facilities were completed only at the very end of 1836, the profits for that year were greater than the cost of the works. At this time the company employed about forty people at the Ballycorus works.[22]

The timing of the new works was just perfect. The year of their construction, 1836, saw a major peak in the profitability of the lead works, with profits reaching no less than £1,820, while in the following year the price of lead slumped again and profits fell to £475, all of which was spent on new machinery.[23] Improvements at the lead works continued over the next few years. In 1839 apparatus for extracting the silver from lead was acquired and a casting house was built for producing sheet lead by casting rather than the more usual rolling method. Casting was preferred by some architects and the installation of this facility allowed the company to offer a greater range of products.[24] In 1840 the price recovered for a while, allowing the works to turn in a massive profit of almost £3,000, though it fell back again fairly quickly.[25]

During this time the company had not altogether given up on the mine at Ballycorus. Mines elsewhere had been abandoned quite readily but somehow Ballycorus held a continuing attraction, partly because its location beside the lead works ensured that there was always a presence of company workers in the vicinity. This opinion was expressed by the chairman of the company in 1858, saying that 'the Ballycorus mine was situated just where the company would place a mine if they professed the power to do so—convenient to the company's smelting house, thus allowing the produce to be smelted and sent to market with the very smallest amount of expenditure'.[26] There were also technical reasons, as the Ballycorus mines were said to be capable of being worked to a considerable depth without machinery. This would mean that the cost of mining the ore would be reasonably low if ore could be found in economic quantities.

From 1837 the company started once again to spend money on investigating the Ballycorus mines, starting with £116 towards the end of 1837 and peaking with £680 in 1839 before waning. Towards the end of 1840 the lead vein was found to split into small branches running deep into the hill; as this would not allow for viable working, the investigation of the mine was suspended again.[27]

The suspension of mining operations at Ballycorus coincided with another slump in the lead market. By 1842 the various lead mines were making losses and, while the Ballycorus works continued to be profitable, the profits were not sufficient to offset the losses at the mines. Despite this, small amounts of money, amounting to about £20 to £80 every six months, continued to be spent on seeking lead at the Ballycorus mine. Late in 1843 the company reported that the mine showed promise of ultimate success, and in 1844 it was revealed that native silver—i.e. pure silver as opposed to its oxide—had been discovered at Ballycorus, together with silver oxide. The quantities were such that it was not immediately obvious whether this would be a viable silver mine. Over the next couple of years further work was carried out on the mine, including the cutting of a new shaft to drain water out of the silver-bearing adit. However, even when silver was produced in 1845 the quantity was small, and it became obvious that the mining of silver would only be viable as part of the mining of the lead vein that accompanied it. The crunch came with the discovery that the lead vein was too narrow and was not capable of being exploited economically, and so neither the lead vein nor the silver could be worked successfully.[28] As a result, the lead and silver veins would still be present below ground today.

The shareholders were not unanimous in their support for the Ballycorus lead works and the expenditure of capital on improving it. On numerous occasions one of the shareholders, Mr Gibbon, voiced his opposition during the half-yearly meetings. In the meeting of January 1843 he spoke out against the company's practice of bringing lead to Ballycorus from one of its mines in Wexford rather than exporting it as ore. The response of other shareholders was that the operations at Ballycorus added value to the ore, and this was reflected in the profits. During that meeting Mr Gibbon stated that he had been opposed to the erection of the smelting works.[29]

Fifteen years after it was built, the horizontal flue needed a major overhaul. The half-yearly meeting for January 1848 was told by the board that Ballycorus had not made a profit for that period, 'it having become necessary to renew the horizontal flue erected fifteen years since, which had become inoperative by the continuous action of the fires during that period, and pending those repairs, now completed, the furnaces could not be worked'.[30]

In the early 1850s the price of lead started to climb again after a slump through most of the 1840s, rising from less than £18 per ton in 1850 to reach £27 in 1856.[31] The lead works at Ballycorus made a loss each year at the end of the 1840s but made a profit in each half-year in the early 1850s. By the middle of the decade the income from the sale of lead and lead products had increased significantly, as a rise in the price of lead put the entire operations for lead production onto a sound financial footing and set the company to consider the investment of a large sum in the radical overhaul of the works at Ballycorus.[32]

COMPANY PROPERTY AT BALLYCORUS IN THE 1840S

By the 1840s the company held some one hundred acres, or forty hectares, of land in the vicinity of the Ballycorus lead mines and lead works, half of which was in Ballycorus and half in the adjoining townland of Rathmichael.[33] On this land there were eleven houses, one of which, in Rathmichael, had a forge attached. The first-edition Ordnance Survey map of the area, dated 1843, shows the earliest detailed picture of the layout of the enterprise.[34] Near the top of the hill is a large expanse of scrub containing Thomas Thompson's Scots pines, now owned by the mining company. Within this area may be seen the original shot works and a number of mine shafts, probably about ten. Towards the lower end of this tract of land are several buildings, most of which were company houses, amounting to seven in number. Some of the mine shafts were just behind these houses.

Going down the hill from this part of the mine works is a road, now known as Mine Hill Lane. The fields here are regularly shaped and the way in which the lane cuts across the fields at an angle suggests that it was comparatively recent and was constructed specially to serve the mines less than forty years before. Towards its lower end, the lane did not even have any boundary but just cut across a field diagonally.

At the bottom end of the lane lay the lead works, where the remains of the works stand today. The number of buildings was considerably fewer then, however, suggesting a much lower degree of work at that time than later in the century. The lead works is labelled 'Ballycorus Mining Company', which is not an accurate title. The map also shows the subterranean flue leading to the elevated chimney of the 1830s.

Elsewhere, the map shows other evidence of mining. On the

eastern side of the hill, in Rathmichael townland, alongside where Puck's Castle Lane was later laid out, three 'Old Shafts' are marked, and on the northern slope a further few 'Old Shafts' may also be seen. As these were not on land that was ever held by the Mining Company of Ireland, they must date from the earlier workings by John Blacker and Richard Redmond which paralleled Thomas Prout's mines at Ballycorus. Three shafts are shown within Rathmichael townland close to the boundary with Ballycorus, while a single shaft is shown at Shankill, close to the boundary with both Rathmichael and Ballycorus.

In 1843 the Ballycorus works received 547½ tons of lead ore from Luganure and 270 tons from the Caime mine in Wexford which yielded 588.2 tons of lead, equivalent to 72% of the ore; this was cast into 10,288 pigs, or ingots, with a sale value of £17 per ton.[35] In that year the Ballycorus works recovered 120kg of silver from the lead ore, which it sold for £1,157.[36]

9

THE RECONSTRUCTION OF BALLYCORUS

In the early 1850s the Mining Company of Ireland set out to enlarge and improve the operations at Ballycorus. Times were changing, and a number of new factors would have been coming into play. With the improvement in building standards there would have been a greater demand for lead for roofing, particularly as Dublin was expanding into the suburbs all around the city. Secondly, the future development of piped water-supplies was becoming more or less a certainty, and this would require a large quantity of lead pipes. Moreover, improvements in transport would potentially make it easier to increase production. Railways had been laid to many parts of Ireland and the local connections from Dublin to Bray via Dundrum and Kingstown were under construction. It would only be a matter of time before the railways would connect closer to the Luganure mines.

The company's first move was to put its legal position in order. A new lease was granted in February 1853, allowing the company to carry out mining at Ballycorus and to develop its smelting works.[1] At the same time, an embarrassing legal difficulty had to be resolved. It transpired that the original lease under which the lead-mining had been carried out was invalid. A 1791 lease of the lands at Ballycorus did not convey the mining rights to the lessee, and so he could not grant them to anyone else. Furthermore, the lease did not have a clause which would allow the lessor to enter onto the lands to explore for minerals or to carry out mining, and therefore he could not grant mining leases either. This had some-how been overlooked for nearly fifty years in the granting of leases, and mining was carried on in happy ignorance of the legal position.[2]

The next move was to reopen the mines at Ballycorus, which had been out of production for some years. This was undertaken in June 1853 and had the benefit of what we would now call a tax incentive, as the mines were declared to be exempt from the pay-ment of rates for the first seven years after reopening.[3] The new lease expected that the mines would be worked and stipulated that the annual rent would be higher if mining was not carried out, but as the difference was only £6 it is obvious that the mines were not reopened simply to reduce the rent. By November of that year more than £300 had been expended on the mine—which, in the light of discoveries in the 1840s, was now being referred to as the Bally-corus Lead and Silver Mine—but it proved to be no more viable at this stage than it had been previously. Losses on the mine varied—sometimes as low as £31 in six months but at other times higher, exceeding £1,400 for the latter half of the years 1857 and 1858, and even higher at almost £2,400 in the first half of 1858.[4] By the end of the seven years of tax exemption it was clear that the mine was not going to return a profit and work was halted in 1860.[5]

Various improvements had been made on an ongoing, incre-mental basis at the Ballycorus lead works, including in 1855 the provision of new machinery for making lead pipes; up to that time pipes could only be manufactured in short lengths, but the new equipment enabled the production of pipes of any length. Never-

theless, the company was aware that the lead works was ageing, becoming worn out and obsolete. The slag hearths, which were used
for recovering lead from poor-quality ore or from slag, were in-
capable of being cleaned properly, and it was estimated that there
was somewhere between £1,000 and £1,500 worth of lead trapped
in the machinery and inaccessible. In 1855 the decision was taken
to engage someone with expertise in lead-processing to reimagine
the lead works, and he proposed significant changes that would in-
volve reconstruction of the works, eliminating the losses in the slag
hearths, making economies in costs and labour, and putting the
lead works in a better working condition.[6]

The result was the rebuilding of the lead works at Ballycorus.
For most of the first half of 1856 work was suspended there while
new machinery was erected along with the buildings necessary to
house it.[7] Over a period of five years or so the improvement of the
works was such as to increase the rateable valuation of the buildings
from £53 to £296, and the total cost of these works was in the order
of £25,000 to £27,000. To finance this undertaking, the company
set up a separate accounting facility known as the Ballycorus Improvement Fund. The cost of the improvements was to be taken
from this fund and was to be repaid through a levy on the profits
from the Ballycorus part of the company's operations. The profits
at this time were higher than they had generally been, but expenditure nevertheless greatly exceeded the flow of finance into the improvement fund during the period of expansion. This would be
normal during any major restructuring and there remained every
likelihood that the company would benefit from the works eventually. By mid-1859 the improvement fund stood with a debt of
£5,700 and, while a further £1,130 towards this fund was available
from the profits by the end of the year, there had been an additional
expenditure of £4,000 in this period, leaving the fund £8,575 in

debit. The sum outstanding peaked at just over £9,000 at the end
of 1860 before reducing again, falling to £3,300 by mid-1864.
Over the next few years this debt was reduced by means of the al-
location of half of the profits from the lead works to the fund, in
addition to money obtained from materials recovered from the new
chimney.[8]

THE BALLYCORUS CHIMNEY AND FLUE

The new chimney and flue were the next, most major and most
spectacular undertaking at Ballycorus during this period of reconstruction in the 1850s. The system built in the 1830s just above
the smelting works had not been the success that had been hoped
for, as it was still too low down in the valley to ensure that poisonous fumes were dispersed away from the district. Lead continued
to be deposited on the local grazing land and the effect on cattle
brought in constant complaints. Despite the reconstruction of the
flue in the 1840s the whole edifice was in poor condition. In July
1857 the chairman told the shareholders that

> 'The chimney of that concern [at Ballycorus] was of very
> old construction, and was now in so tottering a condition
> that their architect had found it necessary to call special
> attention to it. It was probable that the occurrence of a
> severe storm during the ensuing winter would have the
> effect of levelling it to the ground, and if that took place
> they would be coerced to build a new chimney, with this
> additional disadvantage, that these works would be
> thrown idle for six or eight months. He thought it indis-
> pensable that a new chimney should be built, and in the
> best possible manner that modern science can suggest.
> The present chimney was built on old principles, and

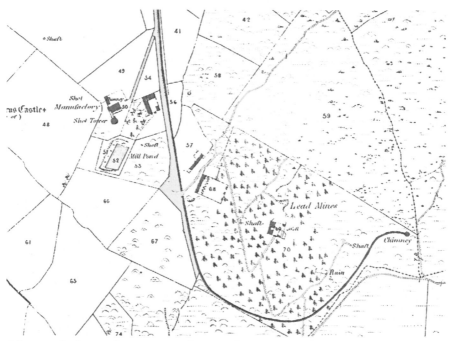

Pl. 19—Ordnance Survey map of 1866, showing line of chimney.

there was wasted and scattered around a great deal of lead which ought to be preserved in the chimney and in the flues connected with it.'[9]

The solution was radical. Operating on the basis of the earlier flue, it was intended to construct a new chimney remote from the works and to connect it by a flue. What made it spectacular was the distance to be travelled. The site of the new chimney was to be at the very highest point of the lands of Ballycorus, at an elevation of 240m above sea level, which is about 150m higher than the works. The chimney itself would add a further 25m to this height.

The flue extends nearly 1,600m from the works, making it just a fraction short of a mile in length. Starting in the middle of the lead works, several separate flues join together, and the resulting main flue passes under the adjoining road and comes up to the sur-

face before running parallel to the road up the hillside to the lands
where the mines had been. In order to do this the company had to
enter into a new lease, as they held land at the lead works and other
land at the mines but merely had a right of way between the two.
To construct the flue necessitated having a lease that permitted this;
it was obtained in October 1857, giving the company 'full power
... to build all such chimneys, flues, buildings or other erections
necessary for the smelting or manufacturing of lead or other ores'.[10]
The construction also meant crossing a farm access lane at the point
where Mine Hill Lane diverges from the country road known as
Sutton's Lane, and to manage this the company had to divert the
farm access over the top of the flue by means of a ramp.

The two sides of the flue are built of granite masonry, while the
arch or vault over the top is of brick along most of its length. Over
the top of the brick vault the flue was covered with a layer to improve insulation so that the temperature would not drop too sig-

Pl. 20—Interior of flue at Ballycorus.

nificantly and to ensure that it was as airtight as possible. What this layer consisted of is uncertain. There is a layer of soil along the top of the surviving lengths of the vault, with grass and other vegetation growing from it. It is possible that this was placed there in the form of grass sods or earth, though soil will often form on top of a building where vegetation has grown over a period of years, but there is a high concentration of pebbles in the soil on the top of the flue, showing that this was not a naturally derived soil arising from the growth of vegetation. It also seems unlikely that any grass sods would have had such a high concentration of rounded pebbles. The most likely scenario is that the top of the flue was sealed with a form of concrete, probably consisting of lime mixed with sand and gravel, and that this concrete has broken down into a stony soil.

In a few places along the length of the flue the vault over the top consists of well-cut granite stones or voussoirs. This occurs wherever a path or roadway crosses the top of the flue, as cut-stone vaults are stronger than brick arches, particularly if the stone is finely cut so that the amount of mortar used is small. This means that if the mortar deteriorates and washes out over the years, the stonework may continue to carry the path or road owing to the close-fitting shape of the stones.

At intervals along the length of the flue doorways were provided, closed by means of heavy iron doors. At the top, where it meets the chimney, there was a huge damper made from an iron plate held up above the flue by a frame. This could be raised or lowered by means of a large wheel to control the draught through the flue.

At the upper end of the flue stands the chimney. This is a graceful construction in coursed rubble stone, mainly granite. Like most older stone-built industrial chimneys, it tapers towards the top and broadens towards the base to add a further beauty to its form. Cantilevered into the sides of the chimney was a flight of granite steps,

Pl. 21—Ballycorus lead works chimney.

many of which remain, though a considerable number have been removed to prevent accidents. The steps lead to a platform below the top, also in granite slabs cantilevered from the masonry. This platform could not have been any closer to the top or the principle of cantilevering would not have worked; the weight of the chimney above the platform ensures that the stones in the platform do not topple over, even with people walking on them. Originally there was a further section of the chimney above the stone, and this was made of brick. This is fairly normal and may be seen in the remaining chimneys at the copper mines at Avoca near Arklow and at the chimney of the shot works that survives at Ballycorus. This brick section may have been the additional section built in 1860 to raise

Pl. 22—Original form of the Ballycorus chimney, with upper section of brick.

the height of the chimney.[11] Rubble stone walls cannot be slender; if the chimney is to taper externally while the internal diameter remains constant, a point will be reached above which the wall of the chimney cannot be built any thinner using rubble. Brick walls could be thinner and so the top portion would be built in brick to maintain a reasonable bore in the chimney. This top brick portion was removed in about 1920 for safety reasons, and photographs of the chimney taken fifteen or twenty years previously show a significant crack in the brickwork.

While the impetus for constructing the chimney and flue came from the need to stop pollution, there was another factor that was considered. The flue at Ballycorus was not new technology, as other similar systems had been built elsewhere and the engineering experience of other smelting works could be drawn upon. It would have been recognised, therefore, that a chimney and flue such as this could contribute finance towards its own construction costs. If lead was being lost into the atmosphere, this was money going up in smoke, and means were sought to recover this lead. It was known that some minerals, such as lead, arsenic and sulphur, would solidify on the walls of a chimney where the smoke met the masonry and cooled down. A longer flue would give more time for a greater amount of the pollutants to solidify on the inside of the flue and be recovered. This is known as a *condenser flue* and had been used at smelting works for lead, arsenic and sulphur since the 1820s. A few years ago, a test was carried out on the material on the inside of the flue at Ballycorus and it was found to contain 30 per cent lead.

The substances that could be recovered from the flue contained not only lead but also arsenic.[12] This was used in medicines and pesticides and thus had a commercial value. Arsenic does not normally exist in the liquid state but will turn straight from solid to gas at 613°C. Any that is present in the lead ore will vaporise at the temperatures in the furnace and go up the flue with the other gases. On the way up the flue it will cool down and solidify on the inside surface.

The furnaces would be shut down, initially twice a year, and the iron doors along the length of the flue would be opened to vent it and cool it down. Workers would then be sent into the flue to scrape the inside to recover the lead. At a meeting of shareholders in July 1860 the chairman of the company said that the results of the first sweeping had been better than expected. They had 'thought that by cleaning the flue after a certain time they might get 50 to 60 tons of lead. At the first cleaning early in 1860 it had given up-wards of one hundred tons of lead', and after this had been pro-cessed they were left with 97 tons.[13] This first sweeping realised a profit of almost £1,500 from the material recovered, a third of which was spent on the construction of a new road on the com-pany's lands and on raising the height of the chimney.[14] From mid-1861 to mid-1862 a further £1,400 was recovered, and in the following year this sum was even greater.[15] By July 1864 the com-pany had recovered some £6,600 from the flue, having paid just £3,000 for the construction of the flue and chimney. The system continued to bring in around £1,500 a year in profit from these sweepings,[16] which was diverted directly into the Ballycorus Im-provement Fund, along with some of the profits of the lead works, until the fund had been paid off.

After the first year or so it was decided that the chimney did not need to be swept twice a year and the decision was taken in January 1862 to carry out the operation only once a year.[17] This decision was not based on the quantity of material deposited in the flue but on the disruption to the operation of the lead works. Each time the flue was cleaned, all work at the plant had to be suspended for three weeks, and the cleaning operation cost £1,000 each time.

A question that has puzzled many people is the purpose of the granite steps and platform and unfortunately this remains a puzzle. The addition of the cantilevered granite steps, the platform at the top and the iron railing would have added to the cost of the chimney and the complexity of construction with no clear purpose. Local resident Phineas Riall mentioned walking to the 'smelting house chimney' in the 1860s but made no mention of climbing it.[18] One suggestion is that it was a viewing platform, either for the general public or as a lookout for military purposes. This seems very unlikely, as the view from the top of the hill is very fine without having to climb the chimney; in the right weather conditions the mountains of Snowdonia may be seen to the east and the Mournes to the north. The additional height would add nothing significant to this. It has also been suggested that the platform at the top would act as a base on which scaffolding could be placed whenever the brickwork above needed to be repaired or maintained. This would also be an unnecessary extravagance, as steeplejacks were fully capable of climbing chimneys of this height and erecting scaffolding where necessary without having permanent platforms and steps. [19]

Following a lecture on the Ballycorus lead mines, an intriguing suggestion was put forward by a member of the audience, who pointed out that many slender steel industrial chimneys have helical vanes that affect the flow of wind around the chimney and prevent it from being blown down in a high wind. Could this have been the reason for the steps on the Ballycorus chimney in its highly exposed hilltop location? Equally, could the effect of the steps on the wind improve the updraft on the outside of the chimney to increase the draw of the chimney by the phenomenon known as the Bunsen effect? Given that the flue is 1,600m long, any improvement in the drawing power that could help the flow of gases to the top might well be beneficial. While these are intriguing suggestions, they do not provide an explanation for the steps at Ballycorus. The vanes on steel chimneys are added to slender chimneys and this is where they function effectively. The chimney at Ballycorus is not slender enough, in relation to its height, for this effect to make any contribution to its stability. As for the Bunsen effect, any air flow up the chimney would be interrupted by the projecting platform, negating any possible benefit from the air being directed upwards by the steps.[20]

The absence of steps from other chimneys associated with mines and factories is notable. There are many mine chimneys in Ireland, such as those at the former Mining Company of Ireland mines at Knockmahon in Waterford and Slievardagh in Tipperary, as well as at the copper mines at Avoca, Co. Wicklow, and Allihies, Co. Cork. Most of these have top sections built of brick and none of them have steps.

THE SMELTING WORKS

The major part of the Ballycorus lead works has always been the group of buildings at the foot of the hill, near the junction of Mine Hill Lane with Ballycorus Road, which make up the smelting works. While the lead works pre-dates the involvement of the Mining Company at Ballycorus, the older buildings that may be seen today date from the period of reconstruction in the late 1850s and early 1860s. This is evident in the style of architecture, which, although relatively plain, includes details such as the slightly pointed arches lined with purple brick and constructed in a style known as the four-centred or Tudor arch.

The buildings that survive on the site of the lead works today

Pl. 23—Buildings at Ballycorus lead works.

include stores for coal, lead ore and other materials. Some of these have been adapted for other uses, such as offices, while others now lack a roof. One line of buildings along the edge of the yard is used for industrial purposes at ground-floor level, while above, at first-floor level, there are workers' cottages that open towards the road, where they have the appearance of single-storey houses. Among the unroofed buildings is one that formerly served for assaying and weighing the silver that was extracted from the lead. Another building that survives, but without a roof, is one of the furnace houses where lead was smelted. This stands apart from the other buildings on the premises, backing on to the small river that runs along the north-western boundary of the lead works site.

One of the most prominent buildings associated with the lead works is the former gate lodge, now in use as a private house. The road was closed off by a timber fence and gateway to regulate traffic

Pl. 24—Gates to Ballycorus lead works, with weighbridge office at left, c. 1900.

in and out of the mining and smelting area. The gates are said to have been closed every evening at 6 p.m., once the lead works finished work for the day.[21] Outside the gate lodge there was a weighbridge in the road, to weigh wagons coming in laden with coal or lead ore and going out with lead products. The wagons were also weighed when empty, so as to calculate the weight of the goods they carried. The gate lodge acted as the office for the weighmaster who operated the weighbridge, and the octagonal bay window to the front allowed him to see vehicles as they approached from either direction.

Leading off the road into the lead works there was an arched gateway. Its granite piers survive, though the arch has been missing for many years, probably because it obstructed the movement of large trucks into and out of the yard.

Adjacent to the gateway is a substantial house known as Ledville,

Pl. 25—Weighbridge office at Ballycorus.

which was built as part of the reconstruction from the late 1850s, probably for use as the manager's or superintendent's house, as it has a distinctly domestic style, though it may have been used as offices for the first twenty years or so until the 1880s. There had been a superintendent's house associated with the lead works from an early period. It is not certain where this was located, but it was probably adjacent to the lead works and is most likely to have been on the site later occupied by Ledville. It was single-storey but with a partial basement, and it was not substantial; measuring 12.5m by 5m externally, it was about the same size as the average small thatched-cottage farmhouse.[22] Ledville is a two-storey house over a basement and is beautifully built, with cut-granite surrounds to the window and door openings. It has a dual aspect, with one frontage directly facing the smelting works while the other looks out on a garden.

Up the hill beyond the works there was a large millpond to store

Pl. 26—Ledville, the manager's house at Ballycorus.

the water necessary for the mill-wheel. There had been a millpond here from the outset, but it was enlarged considerably in 1859 to provide a sufficient water-supply for a new water-wheel.[23] The pond survives, though it has silted up to a significant degree and much of the area is overgrown with reeds. There is an island in the middle and over time it has obtained a picturesque enclosing canopy of trees. According to local tradition, the pond has a floor of brick which, presumably, aided the cleaning out of accumulated silt so that it would continue to store sufficient water to run the mill-wheel. The water was conducted to the works by a mill-race, part of which may still be seen near the gateway to the Roadstone depot above the former lead works.

In July 1861 the chairman reported to the shareholders that costs had been incurred on the construction of furnaces, litharge ma-

chinery, pipe-testing apparatus, a crushing mill and a shed, and
that 'I am happy to tell you that the expenditure of a few hundred
pounds … will terminate expenditure at Ballycorus. We do not
now contemplate any further works there.'[24] Further works were
soon contemplated, however, though they were not substantial. It
occurred to the company that coal was much cheaper in the
summer, when it could be purchased at three, four or even five shillings per ton cheaper than in winter. As the operations at Ballycorus
consumed some 5,000 tons of coal per year, a potential saving could
be made by laying in stocks during the summer and storing them.
A saving of four shillings a ton would save £1,000 a year, and even
a two-shilling saving would amount to £500. Accordingly, it was
decided to spend £700 to erect a coal shed, which would pay for
itself in a very short time.[25]

The Ordnance Survey's map (Pl. 27), surveyed in 1866, shows
the lead works shortly after the completion of the reconstruction.
The buildings on this map are coloured in red, with the exception

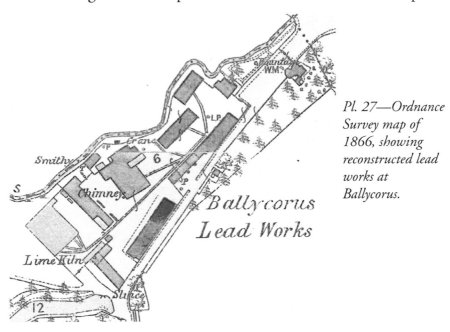

Pl. 27—Ordnance
Survey map of
1866, showing
reconstructed lead
works at
Ballycorus.

of the coal store at the top of the yard, at far left. The paired lines that connect many of the buildings and which run down the centre of the yard represent railway tracks, indicating that the heavy or bulky materials such as coal and lead ore were moved about on wagons that ran on rails and were probably hauled by ponies or mules.

Many of the buildings that were erected in the 1850s and 1860s have now gone, along with buildings that had survived from the earlier periods in the history of the lead works. There was a second furnace house, the site of which is now occupied by the large modern building in the middle of the yard. Beyond this, uphill to the south-west, there was a large building complex built around the old 30ft water-wheel to avail of the power it produced. These included the rolling mill, where sheets of lead were produced, pipe mills, where lead pipes were manufactured, and the pot house, where silver was separated from the lead.

At the far end of the yard, or the upper level, there is a range of buildings in commercial use that have been converted from previous uses as part of the lead works. These include stores, a former limekiln with a water-tank above, a lime house and an office. Nearby, another range of buildings incorporates parts of the walls of the silver refinery and the building where red lead was made for use in the manufacture of anti-rust paint. At the very top end of the complex there is a yard that was originally the coal yard, as the furnaces for smelting consumed a considerable quantity of coal, as has been noted.

There were other buildings on the site that provided amenities for the employees. These included privies—one located at the edge of the yard, backing on to the river, and the other outside the yard on the opposite side of the road; the latter was opposite the workers' houses and would have served them as well as the works. Another facility was a dining room, located adjacent to the main gate, while

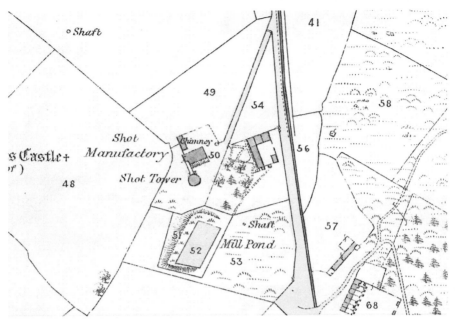

Pl. 28—Ordnance Survey map of 1866, showing new shot works at Ballycorus.

elsewhere on the site there was a bathhouse. In later years one of the rooms in the works was allocated to the Ballycorus Band; the Mining Company facilitated this band, much as did many other industries at the time, a tradition still represented today by Britain's Grimethorpe Colliery Band and Black Dyke Band.

It is not known for certain who the architect was who designed the new buildings at the lead works in the 1850s. It is likely that it was Hugh Carmichael, who was the designer of the shot works, as discussed below. There is no obvious reason why the company would use different architects for the two sites, particularly as they were under construction at the same time. On the other hand, the style of the buildings at the shot works is different from that at the lead works, though this does not necessarily indicate that they were designed by different architects.

As part of the reconstruction the company built a new shot

works. In July 1857 the shareholders were told that 'the shot tower
… was a very old building. They were not enabled to supply one
half the demand for shot, and the directors thought it was essen-
tially necessary that a new tower be built, or the present one be
considerably modified.'[26] The decision was to go for a new shot
tower on a new site. The architect was Hugh Carmichael of the
partnership Carmichael and Jones. The company advertised for
tenders for the construction of the tower in August 1858, advising
potential applicants that the plans and specifications could be seen
'at the offices of Messrs. Carmichael and Sons, Architects'.[27] This
suggests that it was Carmichael rather than his partner Alfred Gre-
sham Jones who was the designer. This supposition is further sup-
ported by the change of architects for the design of the manager's
house in 1862, as Hugh Carmichael had died by that time while
Jones lived for a further fifty years.[28]

Pl. 29—Ballycorus shot works, c. 1900.

Pl. 30—Shot tower at Ballycorus, c. 1900.

Pl. 33—The original manager's house, now Ballycorus Grange.

though not the design that was built.[38] Apart from differences in the design of the windows in the front elevation as shown on the drawings as compared with the house as built, the two chimney-stacks in the house are orientated differently, indicating a difference in the internal layout.

After twenty years the company decided to relocate the manager to Ledville, adjacent to the works.[39] It is probable that this move reflected the state of the Mining Company of Ireland at that time. The price of lead had been falling for a while, resulting in losses at Luganure and sometimes also at Ballycorus. In 1881 some employees at Luganure were let go, including the manager, purser and paymaster.[40] In these circumstances it is likely that the decision to move the manager to Ledville and to dispose of the former manager's house was made in order to reduce costs. In November 1883 the company advertised the old manager's house to be let to a ten-

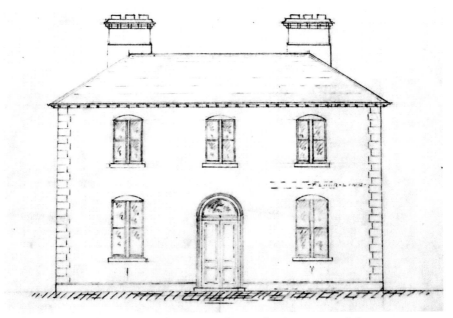

Pl. 34—Unbuilt design by Charles Geoghegan for the manager's house.

ant.[41] It then became known as Ballycorus House, and in the early twentieth century this name was changed to Ballycorus Grange.[42]

RAILWAYS AND RATHMICHAEL ROAD

At the time of the reconstruction of the lead works at Ballycorus the question of transport was also addressed. Even as work started on the new lead works it must have been evident that railways would soon emerge to help the movement of lead ore from Luganure. By the mid-1850s railway lines had been constructed out of Dublin in all directions and two lines had opened leading to Bray, one via Kingstown (now Dún Laoghaire) and the other via Dundrum. One of these, the Harcourt Street line via Dundrum, had a station at Shankill, only a little over two miles from Ballycorus; this is now the Station House office suites on Station Road, off Dublin

Road. Plans were afoot to continue the railway beyond Bray to Wicklow and this had potential for carrying ore. This idea came to fruition in the early 1860s and the new line ran inland beyond Wicklow through Rathdrum, opening between Kilcommon, to the north of Rathdrum, and Bray in 1861 and running through to Rathdrum over a substantial stone viaduct opened in 1863. It was now simpler for the mining company to run its ore wagons down the valley from Luganure as far as Rathdrum and to carry the ore by rail to Shankill, and to this end the company negotiated with the Dublin Wicklow and Wexford Railway to open a siding at Shankill by the beginning of 1862.[43]

On the short route from Shankill station to the lead works there was one major hill, known locally at the time as Cassidy's Hill. This led up from the Bride's Glen and, while it was not a long hill in comparison with some in the Wicklow area, it was significant for its gradient of 1 in 6. In April 1860 two ratepayers applied to the grand jury to have a new road constructed leading off Ballycorus Road towards Shankill station in order to bypass Cassidy's Hill.[44] It is no coincidence that one of the ratepayers was Robert Heron, secretary to the Mining Company of Ireland. The grand jury was the body responsible for the construction and maintenance of roads, and certain other duties, prior to the establishment of the county councils in 1898. Periodic sessions known as 'presentments' were held to allow ratepayers to put the case for works to be carried out by the grand jury. The engineer who reported on the request for the new road commented that the present line of the road was 'badly engineered, passing over one of the worst hills in the county … badly fenced in several places so as to make it an inconvenient, unsafe and disgraceful thoroughfare through the country'. The grand jury was also told that the present road was 'so steep that it requires an additional horse to draw a load of corn 15 cwt up it to

Ballycorus and that district ... there is a danger bringing a heavy load down it'.

Shortly after the opening of the Harcourt Street railway line, the landowner at Shankill, Sir Compton Domvile, had laid out a new private road from what was then the new Shankill station, on Station Road, towards a part of his land that would otherwise have been re-mote from the station, near the present Rathmichael Church. This road was an instant success and, despite being a private road, was used from the outset by local people.[45] As a result, it was taken over as a public road and is now known as Stonebridge Road.

What the Mining Company and others proposed in 1860 was that Sir Compton Domvile's new road should be connected to Bal-lycorus Road by means of a new road to be built by the grand jury. The result of this lobbying was the building of Rathmichael Road, a gently curving road with easy gradients that runs for just over a kilo-metre or, in the measure of the time, 227 perches. While this leads to Domvile's Stonebridge Road, which has a fairly steep hill, the total rise in levels coming from Shankill station is not as bad as on Cas-sidy's Hill, as the old route involved descending a considerable dis-tance to Loughlinstown and having to climb up again to Shankill station. The new road was built during 1861 and would have been ready for use by the time the railway connection between Rathdrum and Shankill was completed.

In 1867 the Mining Company invited tenders for the carriage of lead and other goods between the Ballycorus works and Dublin city.[46] The contract would be for one year and it seems likely that contracts were awarded annually. It may seem strange that the company would seek such a contract, given that the railway was available and reason-ably close, but it may be assumed that the successful bidder for the contract could have the option of using the railway for part of the journey; the destination of the goods would have been to various parts of the city, and transportation from Harcourt Street station to various points around the city would have been required.

In 1881 a new railway was proposed that would have run near to Ballycorus, though what use it might have been to the mining company is unclear.[47] The proposal was for a light railway or an electric railway running from 'the south side of the Dodder, opposite Upper Rathmines', suggesting that it would have its terminus somewhere around Dartry, or perhaps at a link with the Harcourt Street line at Milltown. The route would then travel via Ballinteer, Stepaside, Golden Ball, Ballycorus, the Scalp, Enniskerry and Dargle Bridge. From there a branch would run to Bray, while the main line would run through Kilmacanogue, Glen of the Downs, Delgany, Altidore, Roundwood, Annamoe and Laragh, terminating at Glendalough. There would also be a branch to Newtownmountkennedy. The possibility of using electric power was thought to provide a potential saving on fuel. The first electric railway had been demonstrated just two years previously at the Berlin Trade Fair by Siemens, and in the following year William A. Traill managed to get an act of parliament for the Giant's Causeway, Portrush and Bush Valley Railway and Tramway Company, which became the first railway in the world to be powered by hydroelectricity.[48] The engineer for that project was Edward Price, who in 1881 proposed the electric railway from Dublin via Ballycorus to Glendalough.[49] No more was heard of this project, which had some potential for providing a new route for the transportation of lead ore from the mines at Glendalough to the smelting works at Ballycorus.

WORKERS' HOUSING

From the outset the Mining Company of Ireland had houses for its workers, some of which had been built by George Casson before

the Mining Company had bought the mines. In 1848, a little before the start of the reconstruction work at Ballycorus in the 1850s,
the company had seven houses at Ballycorus and another four on
its adjoining lands at Rathmichael, one of which had a forge attached.[50] The building work at Ballycorus coincided with reorgan-
isation at the Domvile estate at Rathmichael and the Mining
Company ceased to have any interest in land there. The four houses
and the forge were demolished.[51]

At Ballycorus the new construction work included houses for the
workers; for instance, £169 was expended in 1860 for the provision
of new cottages for workmen.[52] It is not possible now to be sure how
many houses there were at any one time, but it would seem that
about seven houses were built in addition to others within the lead
works buildings. The position is a little clearer in the 1880s, when
the company had about twenty houses, including the manager's
house. There were also six rooms occupied by workers, presumably
what we would now call bedsitters or studio apartments.[53]

Pl. 35—Workers' housing above the lead works at Ballycorus.

This was the peak in the number of workers' houses at Ballycorus. After this the numbers declined slightly, and one or two of the houses fell into ruins. At the turn of the century the company had twenty dwellings, of which three were vacant.[54]

BALLYCORUS NATIONAL SCHOOLS

During the major reconstruction of the lead works at Ballycorus it became obvious that if the company was to operate successfully it would need clerical workers as well as industrial operatives. Schooling was not compulsory at the time, however, and schools were few and far between, with the result that literacy was poor among the local population. The company needed employees who would check goods received and dispatched and could perform basic clerical functions, but the clerk of the mining company, William Harold, had some difficulty in finding any man or boy amongst the workers at Ballycorus who could read or write well enough to act as tallyman at Kingstown (now Dún Laoghaire), where coals, bricks etc. were imported.[55] The position is best summed up in the words of the District Inspector for National Schools, Cornelius Mahony, who visited the district in August 1859 and reported to the Commissioners for National Education.[56] He stated that there was a very great necessity for building a schoolhouse here, and went on to say that

'there is a large and crowded population in the immediate vicinity of the site unprovided with any means of education except the schools at Loughlinstown which are too far away for most of the children, and those at Glencullen which are also remote and difficult of access, so that all the smaller children and most of those who have reached the ages of 10 and 12 years have practically no scheme at all. And their

number is very considerable. It appears from a return very
carefully prepared by the Superintendent of the Lead
Works that there are nearly 200 children (73 males and 113
females) within a radius of half a mile and close upon 250
(103 males and 142 females) within a radius of a mile. Upwards of 100 heads of families are employed in or in connection with the lead works either permanently or
occasionally—and without taking account of those who
have fewer than 3 children, I find that 33 of them have an
aggregate 165 children between them. Judging by the oc-
cupations of the parents a more regular attendance may be
expected than is generally found in rural schools. For none
of them hold land; and few of them can find other occu-
pation for the younger children, or in fact for any of them
until they arrive at an age for hand work. A single fact pain-
fully attests how much education is wanted in the locality.
Out of some 130 men who are paid wages in connection
with the lead works not more than 3 or 4 are able to sign
their names to the receipts. I would anticipate from the
abilities and zeal of the Directors of the Company and of
their offices that this—besides being one of the most
needed—may also be one of the most successful schools in
Ireland.'

The Mining Company held a lease of nearly fifty acres of land
adjacent to the lead works and to the east of it, and a site here was
suggested for the school. The land was outside Ballycorus into the
next townland of Rathmichael, and the company's lease was for
sixty years from the ground landlord, Sir Charles Domvile. The
company felt that at least £100 would be required to establish the
school and offered more if it were needed. While retaining nominal
ownership, the Mining Company believed that it should be run as
a model school rather than be controlled by the company.

Pl. 36—The former Ballycorus National Schools.

The establishment of the school received the approval of the parish priest but not that of the Church of Ireland rector, Dr Hunt, who considered the parish schools to be quite sufficient, as the rector of Monkstown parish had a school close to the lead works. At this time the neighbouring parish of Tully, just across the stream from the Ballycorus works, was administered by the rector of the parish of Monkstown, and a school had been established in a house now known as Kingston Grove on Ballycorus Road.[57] The District Inspector of National Schools believed that Dr Hunt would use his influence to prevent the children of his congregation from attending Ballycorus National School if it were established. It does not seem that this was felt to be a major problem, as the inhabitants of the Ballycorus area were not, by and large, members of the Church of Ireland.

Approval for the two schools—one each for boys and girls—was granted and they were completed by early 1862 to the designs of James Higgins Owen, Principal Architect to the Board of Public Works.[58] In May of that year the Commissioners for Education approved the Mining Company's application for aid towards the salaries of the two teachers: Joseph McCarroll, who was to receive £38 a year, and Margaret McCarroll, who would receive £36.[59]

In his chairman's address at the half-yearly meeting in July 1862, Francis Codd announced that the company would provide a house for the schoolmaster at Ballycorus.[60] He then made the following, somewhat condescending, comment:

'I tender you my warmest congratulations upon the result of our school there. It has been only a few weeks opened, and so highly are its advantages appreciated that it already has about 100 children, in constant attendance, rescued from idleness and vice, and training up to be good servants, I hope, for use in their different departments. Gentlemen, there is even a more agreeable subject for congratulation than this. We find that already 25 of our adults—workmen—themselves the fathers of families, have, without solicitation or any inducement upon the part of officers of the company, quitted the public-house in the evening, and are attending the evening schools, learning to read and write, and preparing themselves for advancement in their respective walks of life. An able and experienced gentleman is at the head of our smelting department at Ballycorus. He has been accustomed to workmen all his life, and the conducting of large establishments in England and elsewhere. He has assured us that the change in the conduct and character of the people and the establishment—the fathers, mothers and children—since the establishment of that school, is a perfect marvel, and he anticipates that in a very short time its effects will be so patent to everybody that we shall be obliged to enlarge our school accommodation for the number of persons who will apply to us for education. We find that the best clerks in our establishment are young men who have been reared or connected in these schools and promoted for good conduct and merit to clerkships in our offices. There is only one place—at the Seven Churches [Glendalough]—where we have no schools, but we have made arrangements with the Commissioners of National Education to establish a school there also. The entire expense to which the company has been put for all this good is £170, as a contribution towards building the schools, and about £30 a year, to pay a schoolmaster.'

Ballycorus National Schools remained in use for over a century. The Mining Company retained its function as patron at least for its remaining time at Ballycorus lead works. The schools remained long after this, though, and only closed in 1965, coinciding with the opening of the new national school at Kilternan for the Roman Catholic parish of Sandyford. The remaining dozen pupils and the last teacher at Ballycorus transferred to this school, Our Lady of the Wayside, on the Glencullen Road.[61] The former schoolhouse is now a private house and is called Victoria Lodge.

SEVEN CHURCHES NATIONAL SCHOOLS

Following the success of the schools at Ballycorus, the Mining Company set about establishing schools to serve the children of the Glendalough and Glendasan area. At the time when the company had acquired its mining rights in that area there was one school in the locality, situated at Brockagh.[62] It was run by a teacher named Pierce Ryan and the room in which it was held was of poor quality. About twenty-four pupils attended the school and the teacher

earned about £2 a year in 1825. The difference between this
teacher's pay and the pay given to the teachers at Ballycorus is partly
due to the difference of almost forty years between the dates to
which these salaries refer. That said, the teacher at Brockagh in
1825 was amongst the lowest-paid in the county at that time. The
school would have been what is generally called a hedge school, established by a teacher often without any teaching qualification and
limited education, who charged a small fee to the pupils who attended and who, in turn, were from poor families.

Soon after the introduction of the national school system in
1831, St Kevin's National School was established at Brockagh, and
this is shown on the first-edition Ordnance Survey map of 1838.

The Mining Company evidently did not consider that there
were sufficient school places in the area in which they were working
at Glendalough, and in 1862 they came to an agreement with the
Commissioners for National Education that schools would be provided 'in the most central part of the Seven Churches'—which probably meant that they would be accessible to both valleys,
Glendalough and Glendasan.[63] The school building was erected at
the lower end of the Glendalough valley, not far from its junction
with Glendasan, and is still to be seen on the northern side of the
road, a little beyond the entrance to the round tower and cathedral
adjacent to the Glendalough Hotel. The former school building
was virtually identical to the Ballycorus school and must have been
designed by the same architect, James Higgins Owen. The house
for the schoolmaster was completed in 1864 and was designed for
the company by Charles Geoghegan, who had designed the manager's house at Ballycorus.[64]

The schools at Glendalough came under the same school inspector as Ballycorus, Cornelius Mahony, who had reported on the opposition of the Church of Ireland rector to those schools. Mr

Pl. 37—The former Glendalough National Schools.

Mahony reported in 1863 that[65]

> 'Two schools at the Seven Churches, for which grants were made in a former year, are just completed. Judging by the success of kindred schools erected by the same company ("mining") at Ballycorus, and the liberality with which the best agencies of instruction will be provided, these schools would be eminently successful, but they are likely to encounter a formidable opposition, which may leave them at least comparatively inoperative for some time to come.'

James Patterson, Head Inspector for the district that included the Mining Company's schools at the Glendalough, Knockmahon and Slievardagh mines, singled out the company for its management of schools:[66]

'In every district there are some [distinguished schools], and the fruits are seen in the superior orderliness and efficiency of the schools. There are various ways in which managers benefit their schools ... but yet are far from being so generally followed as they might be. ... The directors of the Mining Company of Ireland, "with a view to encourage good conduct and attention to studies on the part of the children frequenting the schools at their establishments ... grant the following premiums at Christmas of every year, viz.:—To the boy who, for the previous year, shall have proved himself most deserving in good conduct and improvement in studies, the sum of three guineas; to the next deserving two guineas; and to the third, one guinea; and a similar grant in the case of girls. The Board reserve to themselves the power of withholding any premium in case of insufficient merit in any of the classes. All the masters employed in the company's schools are enjoined to afford every possible facility to the local clergy to visit the schools; and at all times manifest towards them the utmost courtesy and respect". The effect of this encouragement given to their schools by the directors of the Mining Company is, that the answering of the pupils, in such of the schools as I have examined, equalled that of the pupils in the model schools.'

The Mining Company was proud of its schools, as is evident by their reports and the awards given to pupils. In July 1864 the chairman, in addressing the half-yearly meeting of the company, said that he attached great consequence to the company's schools at Glendalough, Ballycorus, Knockmahon and Slievardagh, and gave his opinion that[67]

'They were cradles of industry and order, and the nursery of man's progress. ... they had determined to give to the

Pl. 38—Mine adit at Luganure, 1856.

It is not clear where the names for the various mines came from. Some, such as Luganure, Ruplagh and Fox Rock, were probably local names for specific parts of the landscape, but it is not known who the Hero was. For that matter, who was Moll Doyle?

These lodes in running north–south tended to appear more than once. Four separate levels, known as 'Shallow adit', 'Weaver's level', 'Deep adit' and 'Richard's adit', had been cut into the Luganure lode from the north, but it had become difficult to keep these workings free of water and a scheme had been devised to dig a long tunnel away from the mine to come out further down the valley so as to allow for natural drainage by gravity. The scheme was abandoned after several years of work, however, when it became obvious that the amount of cutting involved was too great and would take too long.

By the end of 1853 lead had been found at the head of the Glendalough valley and began to be worked on a significant scale, show-

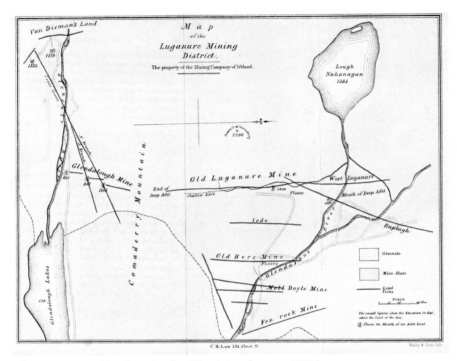

Pl. 39—Veins of lead ore in the Glendalough area, 1856.

ing considerable promise.[1] The Mining Company's agent in the
Glendalough district was Captain Clemes, and his son, who was
working with him, succeeded in finding the location of the lead
veins on the Glendalough side of Camaderry Mountain.[2] The mine
produced about £2,200 worth of lead after all costs were paid and
£737 of this was ploughed back into extending the mines, with
Captain Clemes reporting that the prospects were 'of a cheering
description'.[3] During 1855 the company began to carry out significant construction works at the head of the Glendalough valley, including the erection of a new crusher and machinery for raising
and dressing the ore. The productivity of the mines had increased
rapidly by this stage, with a surplus of £6,100 in the second half of
the year, from which more than £1,000 was spent on the new

works. A significant factor in the increase in productivity was the improvement in the price of lead, reaching levels of between £15 and £16 per ton in comparison with £7 previously.[4]

At this stage a significant problem arose. The company had invested £4,000 in acquiring the mineral rights in the Glendalough valley, but only the mineral rights; others had title to the land for other purposes, such as agriculture. This meant that to provide access to the mines at the head of the valley and to erect buildings the company had to negotiate rights to the land with those who occupied it. As might be expected, the landholders, realising that they were in a strong bargaining position, looked for extravagant payments for the use of the land. Three company directors— Thomas Bewley, Francis Codd and Robert R. Guinness—took the matter in hand. In an inspired move, they found a way around this problem by having a boat built so that they could extract the ore from the mining area across the length of the upper lake without having to construct a road or any buildings to dress the ore. Faced with the prospect of levying a realistic price for the use of the land or getting nothing at all, the landowners capitulated and came to an agreement. As a result, more than three miles of roads were laid out, leading to the head of the Glendalough valley, and work proceeded on the erection of buildings and other facilities for the mines in that area.[5]

The lode being worked in the valley at Glendalough turned out to be the same Luganure lode that was being exploited on the far side of Camaderry Mountain, and in 1856 the two mines were connected through the mountain so that they could be worked as a single mine.[6] The company's agent was again given credit in the annual report for this achievement, which was described as 'an undertaking of magnitude and difficulty'. Like its counterpart in Glendasan, the Luganure lode in Glendalough proved to be a very

Luganure Lead Mine, County Wicklow, Ireland.

Pl. 40—Mine workings at Glendalough, 1859.

valuable source of lead ore. This was a fortunate state of affairs, as the workings to the north of the mountain were becoming difficult to operate.

From a high point in 1855 lead prices fell significantly, though this meant reduced profit rather than loss at Luganure, amounting to £3,457 in the latter half of 1856 and £3,091 in the first half of 1857.[7] In the first of these periods the company had spent £930 draining the mines, constructing watercourses and connecting the two mines, while in the second period £635 was spent on extending the dressing floors and erecting buildings for the accommodation of the mine workings, cottages for the mine workers and houses and out-offices for the company's farm tenants, as the company was now a ground landlord as well as a mining company. In addition, a stamping machine and water-wheel were under construction.

Pl. 41—Crusher house and workings at the head of the Glendalough valley.

The new route through Camaderry Mountain ran for a total of some 2.5km and allowed the mines in Glendasan to be drained downhill into Glendalough rather than having to be pumped out. It also meant that the ore from the Luganure lead vein could be brought out at Glendalough, which was at a lower level, thereby allowing the advantage of gravity in moving the material. Once it had been processed at the new dressing floors and crushing mill, the ore was brought along the road constructed by the company leading to the monastery at Glendalough, and from there it went down the valley to Rathdrum, where from 1862 it met the railway.

The Mining Company now commenced a new forestry venture, reclaiming a substantial area of the hillside at Glendalough and planting it with trees. According to its own reports it was planting larch and fir, though it was really larch and pine, as at that time Scots pine trees were usually known as Scotch fir. By the middle of

Pl. 42—Adit at Fox Rock.

1857 it had planted some 150,000 trees.[8] Six years later the amount of hillside reclaimed covered 60,000 hectares or 150,000 acres, and some 750,000 trees had been planted.[9] This amounted to 100,000 trees a year, and to facilitate this the company had established a tree nursery in the valley. The planting was seen as providing a great scenic attraction, as well as supplying timber for use as pit props, timbering for the entrances to mines and for any other project associated with the mines that needed timber. It was also anticipated that within a few years the forests would yield an income from sale of timber to offset the cost, which amounted to £8 per acre or £20 per hectare, including the cost of fencing. Furthermore, there were about another 200 acres of land in the hands of the company that were to be given over to forestry. In the 1860s the company built a sawmill on its lands to the north of the monastic ruins at Glendalough, powered by water from the adjacent Glenealo River.[10]

Pl. 43—Proposed offices, stables and stores at Glendalough.

Into the 1860s additional facilities were provided at the mines in Glendalough and Glendasan, while the search for more lead deposits continued. New houses were provided for the miners during 1859 and 1860, and the facilities for dressing ores were improved.[11] The new houses included twenty that were built on the southern side of the Glendasan River, amongst which was a terrace of eight houses that later became known as Fiddlers' Row, apparently because of the number of musicians who lived there.[12] The company planned new buildings to serve the booming mine workings at Glendalough, engaging the architect Charles Geoghegan to design a manager's house, stables, stores and offices on a site just beyond the hotel at Glendalough, between the road and the river, although these were not built in the end.[13]

Early in 1861 the ongoing prospecting in the area provided positive results when a new lode of lead ore was discovered at Fox Rock, on the northern side of the valley of Glendasan, opposite the Hero mine. The chairman reported to the shareholders that this lode 'in size and quality is entitled to the appellation of a mine ... from which we anticipate a very considerable advantage'.[14]

During the 1850s and early 1860s the Mining Company found

itself in frequent litigation with the occupiers of land in the vicinity of the mines at Luganure, mainly based on claims that cattle were being injured by the vicinity of the lead mines. In his address to the shareholders in January 1854 the company's chairman implied that there was what we might call a 'claims culture' behind these allegations.[15] Eight years later the chairman was delighted to report that 'a tenant who adjoined this mine and had been found very litigious, had been purchased out for £1,000 and the mountain was now entirely the property of the company'.[16]

The new working at Fox Rock proved to be productive. Prospecting continued throughout the area, particularly after 1865, when profits began to rise again. This resulted in the discovery in 1868 of another new source of lead high up above the end of the valley of Glendalough.[17] This was a remote area, accessed with difficulty, and was given the name 'Van Diemen's Land', in reference to the remoteness of the former penal colony, though transporta-

Pl. 44—View of the Glendalough valley from Van Diemen's Land.

tion to Van Diemen's Land had ceased in 1853 and the island had been renamed Tasmania in 1856.

With the increase in productivity at Luganure arising from the new workings at Fox Rock and Van Diemen's Land, combined with an improvement in the market for lead, the company began to improve the facilities in Glendasan and Glendalough again. In 1869 this included new buddles on the dressing floors, the cutting of new watercourses, alterations to a dam at Lough Nahanagan to improve the flow of water for water-power and the extension of works at each of the mines in operation.[18] This work had cost £830 in the second half of 1869, while a larger sum, £914, was spent on improving the access to and from Van Diemen's Land.

The new working at Van Diemen's Land was a little over 1km from the crushing mill and other processing facilities at the head of the Glendalough valley, but it was also well over 200m higher.[19] Initially mules were used to transport goods up to the new mine and, more importantly, to carry the lead ore down for processing. By 1869 it was clear that this mine would be productive and that it would be worthwhile to provide a more efficient system. A common method of bringing the produce of mines to a lower level was the *inclined plane*, which worked on a similar principle to the funicular railways that are common in various tourist spots. Two railway tracks are laid side by side, running in a straight line downhill and at a constant gradient. Wagons on one track are attached to wagons on the other by a chain or cable that runs over a pulley wheel at the top, between the tracks, so that when the wagons on one track are at the top, those on the other track are at the bottom. The wagons full of ore are carried down by gravity, while the chain or cable pulls the empty wagons up from the bottom of the slope. The pulley wheel would have brakes so that the descending heavy wagons do not travel too rapidly.

Pl. 45—Seating for steam engine, Van Diemen's Land.

The inclined plane to Van Diemen's Land was constructed on the southern side of the waterfall which brings the Glenealo River down into Glendalough. The terrain is extremely rugged and before any railway track could be laid the route had to be levelled and cleared to produce a straight, even slope. The work went on through the latter half of 1869 and had been completed by the autumn of 1870.[20] The cost was £2,400—an enormous sum in comparison with the average annual profits from all of the mines in the Glendalough area combined, which sometimes didn't reach that amount.

Unfortunately for the mining company, the completion of the inclined railway coincided with a downturn in the fortunes of the mines in the Glendalough area. In the second half of 1870 the lead ore raised from the mines amounted to 577 tons, as compared to 750–800 tons in a normal six-month period, and this was exacer-

factors led to expansion of credit and reckless speculation, resulting in the collapse of a number of banks and other financial institutions.[3] In January 1867 the chairman of the Mining Company reported to the shareholders that, since the previous shareholders' meeting,[4]

> 'the commercial interests of these countries had been exposed to a financial crisis unexampled for intensity and continuance in the recollection of the oldest merchants. The banking laws were suspended, an arbitrary rate of interest of 10 per cent imposed by order of government, some of the most honoured commercial establishments destroyed, and even large banking concerns, in which the public reposed almost unbounded confidence, were obliged to suspend payment.'

The increased interest rate affected the company badly, as it had made significant borrowings to fund the development of new mines and new buildings and machinery, including a loan of £32,985 from the Royal Bank of Ireland. Nonetheless, at the same meeting the company recorded a profit of £5,657 and declared a dividend of 8 per cent.[5]

From the outset the Mining Company was affected by international events from time to time, particularly where supply of copper or lead was either increased or decreased, leading to changes in the prices on the markets. At the same time as the American Civil War, there was a war between Spain and Chile in 1864, resulting in greater scarcity of copper ore, which brought prices up from a rock-bottom level and enabled the company to sell ore at a reasonable price.[6]

Spain was also the root of a more serious impact on the markets from the late 1860s, however, with far-reaching effects on the Min-

Pl. 46—Interior of an ore hopper at Glendalough.

ing Company of Ireland. In 1852 the Linares Lead Mining Company was established by English entrepreneurs in Spain, followed two years later by the Fortuna Company, which was also English-owned. Investors from other countries, including France, Belgium and Germany, followed suit. These companies began mining lead in large quantities and found that they were able to bring it to the markets at a significantly lower price than British and Irish companies. In the late 1830s lead mines in the United Kingdom, including Ireland, were producing 40 per cent of the world's lead, and through the 1840s and 1850s the output amounted to half of the lead produced in Europe. With the competition from the Spanish lead mines, those in the United Kingdom suffered and by the 1880s their share of the world's lead produce was down to 14 per cent, exacerbated by a decline in the amount of lead ore being discovered and worked in Britain and Ireland.[7] In fact, by 1869 the

APPENDIX 1

REMNANTS OF THE LEAD WORKINGS

The traces of the lead workings in the Glendalough and Bally-corus areas are plentiful; this description does not attempt to list them all, nor to explain them all, but to offer a brief introduction to what may be seen on site today. I must reiterate what I said in the introduction—that any visitor to these sites must treat them with extreme caution. There are many open mines in the Glendasan and Glendalough area and these are dangerous, particularly any

Pl. 48—Spoil heaps at Fox Rock and Moll Doyle mines, Glendasan.

shafts that are open. Fencing, where it exists, may be broken down or rotten, and some shafts have little or no protection. Where there are buildings or other structures, these are often in a precarious state and it is advisable not to climb on any of them, no matter how robust they may seem.

In this description the remnants are taken in five sections: Glendasan, Glendalough, Ballycorus mines, Ballycorus flue and Ballycorus works. Some of the remaining evidence of mining or mineral-working is on private property and nothing in this book should be taken as implying a right of access.

GLENDASAN

The R756 leads westward from the village of Laragh, Co. Wicklow, before dividing at a fork after about 1.5km. The main road runs to the right, slightly north of due west, towards the Wicklow Gap and onward towards Hollywood in west Wicklow. This is the valley of Glendasan, through which flows the Glendasan River, which drains the valley and Lough Nahanagan and which provided water-power for the lead mines in the valley, for pumping water out of the mines, for powering the crushing mills that pulverised the ore and for other purposes.

After a steep climb of about 2.5km the road levels off, and between here and the Wicklow Gap is high moorland scattered with bright white piles of stones—the spoil heaps from the various lead mines. At the point where the valley levels off, a small spur of road runs off the main road for a short distance and provides parking space for a few cars. On the opposite side of the river from this road is a group of ruined buildings and other structures. This is the working area at the Hero mine and is the largest group of mine buildings in Glendasan. Here there are extensive areas paved with cobbles; these are the dressing floors where the rock was broken up to extract the ore. One of the buildings was the crusher, and it is still possible to identify where a water-channel entered the side of the building, where a water-wheel was mounted and was turned by the water to power the crusher.

A smaller valley perched high up on the southern side of Glendasan is the location of the original Luganure mine and spoil heaps from these workings are still visible.

Other remnants in Glendasan include the ruin of a blacksmith's forge. This would have been an essential part of the works, as the blacksmith would have been responsible for the repair and maintenance of machinery, the shoeing of the horses used for transport and for power, and also for keeping the miners' chisels sharp and well tempered.

GLENDALOUGH

The mining area at Glendalough is at the head of the valley, above the upper lake. The miners' road runs from the car park at the upper lake for just over 2km before it meets the beginnings of the lead workings. The mines were high up on the slopes on the northern side of the valley and the spoil heaps are plainly visible. The roadway meets extensive areas of spoil heaps, many of them with flat tops that are paved with cobbles; these are the picking floors or dressing floors where the stone was broken up to extract the ore. Adjacent to the picking floors, at the foot of the slope, there is a small building with a narrow vertical entrance in the middle and with the floor inside sloping towards that opening. This was a hopper, into which the stone extracted from the mine was tipped to be ready for those who were going to break it up on the dressing floors.

Beyond the dressing floors is a line of ruined buildings that
would have held offices, stores and amenities. Standing apart from
that line is the ruin of a larger building. This was a crushing mill
that was powered by water, with a large water-wheel on its southern
side. The action of this mill is described below in the account by
Harry N. Draper. The water-supply to this mill was brought from
a millpond that was created by damming the river a little further
up the valley, and the remnants of this dam may still be seen as a
wall of large stones. In its original form it would have been sealed
with clay to keep it watertight.

Beyond the crusher and the millpond is the head of the valley.
Here the river gushes down the steep slope, while a footpath zigzags
up the northern side of the river towards the mining area known
as Van Diemen's Land. With some imagination it is possible to discern sections of the route of the inclined plane that ran down from
Van Diemen's Land parallel to the river on its southern side. The
line is clearly visible on aerial photographs, though there is nothing
left of the rails or machinery that carried equipment and coal up
to the top and carried ore down to the bottom.

On the moorland at the top of the path a number of spoil heaps
are visible, and amongst them is a stone-built structure that was
the base on which a steam engine sat. This may have provided the
power for pumps used to keep the mines dry.

BALLYCORUS MINES

The visible remains of the mine workings at Ballycorus are all high
on the hillside not far from the chimney. The mine shafts were located on an alignment from the top of the hill near the chimney
downhill towards the west-north-west, following the junction between the granite and the mica schist. They are not in a dead

Pl. 49—Capped mine shaft near the chimney at Ballycorus.

straight line, however, as the junction of the two rocks continues below the surface and is hence not a linear junction but three-dimensional. The shafts are marked on the early Ordnance Survey maps, including the first-edition six-inch map of 1843 and the second-edition map of 1871. The larger-scale 1:2,500 maps published in 1866 and 1909 also show the shafts, and the latter also shows the site of opencast mining.

The opencast mining site is the most obvious remnant on the ground, as it forms a substantial scar along the hillside, with a cut in the centre and the spoil debris on either side. This opencast working was partially backfilled for safety reasons, and thus the original cutting into the hillside is now relatively shallow. At the upper end of this scar the two rock types—granite and mica schist—are plainly visible alongside each other.

The mine shafts at Ballycorus are more difficult to discern, as they all appear to have been capped and grass or gorse has grown over the capping. One shaft is visible near the top of the opencast scar, on its southern side, where it can be seen as a circular depression in the ground about 3m across and about 0.5m or so deep in the centre, with a low mound on its downhill side. In 2017 or 2018 some filming took place near the chimney, and gorse was cleared from a large area to facilitate the production. Within the cleared area there were two or three large circular depressions that exactly correspond with mine shafts marked on the first-edition Ordnance Survey map. As noted in the introduction, no one knows what these shafts were capped with or whether the capping might rot over time and collapse. Any reassurance that the shafts were backfilled with loose rock is undermined by a story told to me from the audience following a lecture, that one of the pine trees on the hill is said to have collapsed vertically into a mine shaft. The widespread presence of gorse on the hillside acts as a deterrent to anyone straying off the well-worn paths, but also conceals any areas where there may be open shafts or other dangers. The safety provided by the gorse disappears periodically in the aftermath of gorse fires.

To the north of the opencast workings, at the top, there is a quarry, which would have provided stone for the construction of the chimney and its flue in the late 1850s. To the south of the opencast workings, at the bottom end, there is a grassy platform near the rough pathway that leads up the hill. This is the location of Richard Brady's original shot tower, built in the 1820s and functioning until the late 1850s.

BALLYCORUS FLUE AND CHIMNEY

Nothing remains above ground of the flue and chimney built by the Mining Company of Ireland in the 1830s. Whether anything remains below ground must remain unknown unless and until investigation takes place.

The flue and chimney built in the late 1850s remain, though the flue is far from intact. This remarkable structure ran all the way from the smelting works in the valley off Ballycorus Road up the hill to the chimney at the top. The length of approximately 1,600m did not run in a straight line. The line is straight from the top end of the smelting works to the hillside above the top of Mine Hill Lane, but after that it sweeps around in a broad curve, turning through nearly 180 degrees before turning back in the opposite direction to meet the chimney on the hilltop.

Some of the flue has been removed by landowners to facilitate access to property. A section at the top was demolished deliberately in 1972 for safety reasons, while other sections have collapsed of their own accord. The rising walls on either side of the flue are constructed of good-quality masonry, consisting of well-mortared granite rubble. The vault over the top of the flue is of brick with a capping of lime-based concrete. The problem is that the concrete element has been broken up by roots, while a great deal of the mortar has leached out from between the bricks in the vault, with the result that the entire top of the flue, where it survives, is in imminent danger of collapse.

There are four places where the vault over the flue was constructed with cut granite to form a stronger capping. This was done wherever a path or roadway was to cross over the flue. The first place is where Mine Hill Lane crosses over the flue at the top end of the smelting works. The second is a farm access at the junction of Sutton's Lane with Mine Hill Lane. The third is above the top of Mine Hill Lane, where the pathway crosses over an underground section of the flue. The fourth is at the south-eastern extremity of

Pl. 50—Flue at Ballycorus prior to demolition in the early 1970s.

the flue, where a pathway used by walkers and horses crosses the flue and where the adjacent section of the flue has collapsed.

In the lower reaches of the flue, alongside Mine Hill Lane, there are openings in the side of the flue. Some of these are bricked up and others are open. These were originally closed off by iron doors and they allowed for access to clean out the flue periodically to recover lead deposits from the inside. Some iron doors were still visible in the 1950s.

The chimney itself is a beautifully built structure, constructed of granite. The flue has been demolished where it approached the chimney, but until the 1950s a substantial iron plate lay on the ground near the chimney. This was the damper that was held on a timber frame and was raised or lowered to govern the draught in the flue. The top section of the chimney is now missing but was of brick, and some of the bricks may still be seen lying on the ground around its base. The steps leading up the chimney originally had an iron railing. Six steps were broken off in 1972 in an attempt to prevent the foolhardy from climbing the chimney.

BALLYCORUS WORKS

The remnants of the lead-smelting works at Ballycorus still occupy the site of the original works that was constructed in 1818–19, though it is unlikely that any of the surviving structures date from that period. Various older buildings may be seen on the site, and these are constructed of stone and with brick dressings around the doors and windows. Most, if not all, of these date from the reconstruction of the works in the late 1850s; some have been refurbished and are in use, while others are derelict and roofless.

The first building seen on approach to the works is the former weighbridge office and lodge with its prominent projecting bay.

Pl. 51—Entrance to Ballycorus lead works.

On the opposite side of the road, just outside the gates to the works, is Ledville, which was the manager's house.

The smelting works is enclosed by a stone wall, with decorative granite piers flanking the gateway; the piers originally carried a Gothic arch that spanned the entrance. Within the works the roofless buildings are concentrated in the lower part of the yard, with the ruined dining room and lumber room immediately to the left inside the gate, beyond which is the roofless assay and weigh house. This latter building has a large archway in the rear wall, now blocked up with concrete blockwork; this is the point at which the flue built in the 1830s exited the yard and it is likely that this blocked archway marks the line of that flue. On the opposite side of the yard is one of the furnace houses, now roofless and very overgrown.

Further into the yard on the left-hand side is a series of two-storey buildings, now in use as offices on the ground floor. This

Pl. 52—Chimney at Ballycorus shot works, 1958.

range of buildings housed stores for coal, ore and other purposes at ground-floor level, while the upper level was accommodation for workers and is still in residential use.

At the top of the yard, and with its own entrance from the road, there is a range of single-storey buildings in business use. These were also built as stores, while the section furthest from the road housed a limekiln.

At the bend in the road above the lead works a gateway leads to a depot for Roadstone, and alongside the road to that depot is the

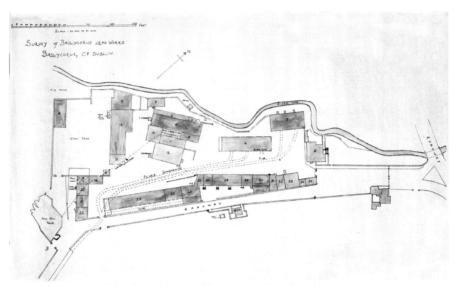

Pl. 53—Survey of lead works at Ballycorus, by Ian Booth.

millpond that provided the water to power the lead works. The pond is now largely populated by reeds but is still fed with water from a weir on the river.

Further up the hillside is the group of buildings that was built in the late 1850s as the shot works. The shot tower was demolished in about 1920 for safety reasons, though the rest of the buildings survive, including the riddle house and an industrial chimney with a brick upper section. The former shot works is within the grounds of a private house and is not publicly accessible.

APPENDIX 2

PROCESSES

As this book is intended for the general reader, I have tried to avoid technical details in the text. However, there are probably some readers who would be interested in how the various systems worked, and these more technical (but still very simplified) descriptions have been relegated to an appendix.

The descriptions below are not my own, though I have rewritten them, paraphrasing them from their original text. The original author was Harry Napier Draper, who happens to have been my great-great-grandfather and who wrote two articles in 1860, one on the mines at Glendalough and the other on the lead works at Ballycorus.[1] My relationship to Harry Napier Draper is just a coincidence; it was only after I had incorporated his information into the text below that I followed him up to see whether he had been related to my grandmother, and he turned out to be her grandfather. Harry N. Draper's father, Carter E. Draper, had come to Ireland from Britain in the middle of the nineteenth century and was a chemist by trade—in the context of scientist rather than pharmacist (though I don't mean to imply that pharmacists are not scientists!). Carter Draper was in partnership with Henry Bewley as Bewley and Draper, chemists, or wholesale druggists and manu-

facturers of mineral waters, in Dublin's Mary Street; Harry followed
him into the business, which he carried on until his death in the
1890s. Harry's younger brother was Carter Draper, County Surveyor for the western division of Galway in 1878–82, following
which he was appointed County Surveyor in Wicklow.[2]

MINING

*[Harry Napier Draper's account of a visit to the lead mines at Glen-
dalough, probably in August 1859[3]]:*
Next morning I started to see the mine … here I met the miners
by the dozens, going to their work; here their wives and daughters
carrying their breakfasts, and the candles with which they light the
mine; and every now and then I passed neat cottages, with patches
of flower garden in front. … The first objects which attract attention at the mouth of our lead mine are a very large water-wheel,
turned by a mountain stream, which rushes down the ravine in
front, and several immense heaps of what appear to be fine white
gravel, but which is really the debris of the mine. Further on, we
come upon several men busily engaged with hammers upon a huge
heap of glistening stone, which is not difficult to tell is the lead ore.
But to see everything, and not to bring away merely a confused
idea of the whole, we must begin at the beginning.

The mine would hardly repay us the trouble and inconvenience
of getting there. All that could be seen would be the miners cutting
away at the rock with their pickaxes to remove the lead, contained
in quartz. They would then select those pieces that contained a sufficient amount of lead to be worthwhile sending to the surface.

The miners are not paid by the hour, nor by the amount of ore
that they send to the surface. Instead, the mining company pur-
chases ore from the miner once it has been dressed and processed

Pl. 54—Picking floor at the Hero mine, Glendasan.

ready for smelting and the price reflects the market price for lead at that moment. From the price paid for the ore the company deducts the price of the implements used and the cost of dressing the ore. This method benefits everyone. The company does not pay for unremunerative labour, while the miner shares the profits of the work with the mining company. This system is only in operation when miners are working on ore deposits, as all of the costs of exploration, opening up a mine and other preliminary operations are paid for by the company.

The product of the mining is a mix of quartz and galena, which is the lead ore. This is placed in wagons running on railway track and within the mine they are hauled by mules, with each mule drawing three wagons.[4] There are two parallel tracks and once the wagons have emerged from the mine two pairs of wagons are attached to each other by a chain that passes over a pulley at the top.

In this way the pair of wagons that are full of ore descend their railway track and in so doing they pull up the empty wagons to the entrance of the mine. The descending wagons pick up sufficient speed on the slope that their momentum carries them across level ground to the two-storey shed in which the crushing machine is located, and they enter the shed at the upper level.[5]

Separation of ore from rock

The crushing machine acts relentlessly, crushing the galena into fragments with as little difficulty as coffee beans in a grinder. On the outside of the crushing mill is a large water-wheel, which drives two iron cylinders, moving in opposite directions by means of cogwheels driven by the water-wheel. The two cylinders are case-hardened to give their surfaces the strength of steel and they are mounted so closely that a pencil passing between them would emerge as a flat band. The two cylinders are kept together by means of a lever attached to one cylinder, at the other end of which is a heavy weight or 'bob', pressing the cylinder towards its companion while allowing a certain amount of give or flexibility.

The ore is fed from above through a hopper, descending in a steady, gradual stream between the cylinders, where it is ground to fragments. The effort required for this process ensures that it is not done rapidly and some of the ore is not crushed sufficiently. Beneath the rollers the ore falls into a tubular sieve set at an angle. The well-crushed ore falls through the mesh, while the imperfectly crushed ore lands in a bucket at the end, from where it is returned to the upper floor to repeat the process. The well-crushed ore is swept by an attendant boy into a wooden gutter or channel.

The ore that emerges from the crusher is still a mix of quartz and galena and the separation of the two takes advantage of the significant difference in the density of the two materials. The crushed ore was swept into the tail-race of the mill-wheel, where the water exited to return to the river. Here in this channel the swift-moving water acted with force on the crushed ore, moving the particles with the current, and before long the crushed ore is separated according to its weight, with the lighter grains moving further. Towards the upper end would be found lumps of galena and along the course of the channel these would get progressively smaller; after an interval the finer particles of galena are found to be mixed with quartz grains, while further still along the channel there is only quartz. At intervals along the channel there were openings leading into shallow tanks, and men with instruments resembling rakes without teeth were in position alongside the channel to move the galena into these tanks.

Those parts of the crushed ore that are still a mixture of quartz with galena would be transferred to oblong boxes which would then be shaken. This shaking action separates the quartz fragments, which, being lighter, rise to the surface and are removed.

Once the galena has been cleansed of all the particles of quartz and other minerals it is placed in heaps, each of which represents one miner's share. Once it has been weighed it is transferred into boxes, which are securely padlocked ready to be conveyed to the smelting works.

SMELTING

[A visit by Harry Napier Draper to the lead works at Ballycorus, c. 1859[6]]:
On arrival at Ballycorus from Glendalough the ore was examined to determine its water content, as the finely crushed ore can hold a significant amount of water. The quantity of lead in the ore was then determined, followed by the percentage of silver. The ore was then stored in ore houses. These preliminary investigations were

Pl. 55—Ballycorus lead works, c. 1900.

undertaken in the assay office, which was located near the entrance to the yard and adjacent to the ore houses.

The ore is removed from the ore house to the furnace for smelting. The smelting is carried out in a *reverberatory furnace*. In this type of furnace, the ore is placed on a slightly dished surface that is raised up above the floor of the building and above which is a brick vault. The fire is at one end of the furnace and the chimney at the other, and the flames travel over the top of the ore on their way to the chimney, so that the heat is mainly radiated from the brick vault, while a great deal of air travels over the ore with the flames.

The galena is lead sulphide, containing twenty-one parts of lead to four parts of sulphur by weight. When the ore is heated to red-hot state it will react with the oxygen in the air that is passed over it to produce lead sulphate, while further treatment will convert the mix to sulphurous acid and molten lead. The process is not

Pl. 56—Smelting house at Ballycorus.

straightforward and depends on skilled workers raking the ore to subject each part of the ore to the heat and oxygen. Over an eight-hour period a furnace will change about two tonnes of galena into molten lead and gaseous sulphurous acid. A plug is removed from the centre of the dished surface to allow the molten lead to pour away into the chamber below, from where it is ladled into moulds to form pig lead.

Despite the care taken to separate the galena from the parent rock or the quartz, there will always be some quartz left in the mix and this will be left in the furnace as slag. Nevertheless, this will still have a value, as it will still contain a significant amount of lead. This is extracted by mixing it with lime and heating it in a blast furnace. The lead that results from this process is not of as good a quality as the lead from the reverberatory furnace, but it is good for making lead shot, as it is somewhat harder.

Separating silver

Even after the smelting process the lead will contain some impurities, but the only one that is of significance is silver. The quantity of silver in lead varies according to the locality where it is found and could be 100 parts per million or 10,000 parts per million, and in some cases the proportion is so high that the lead is neglected for the sake of the silver. At Ballycorus, however, the proportion is 140–340 parts per million, or between 0.14kg and 0.34kg per tonne.

From time immemorial precious metals have been separated from less-valuable metals by cupellation. This process is based on a difference between the lead and silver when the metal is heated to a red heat and a strong current of air is passed over it; the lead will oxidise while the silver will not. This is a very tedious process and requires a lot of fuel and hence would not be economically viable where the proportion of silver in the lead is small, even though the lead itself can be recovered, either as the oxide or reduced back to metallic lead by smelting with coal. However, there is another reason why this process would be carried out. A small percentage of silver in the lead makes the lead hard and brittle and not suited to many of the uses to which it would normally be put. For example, lead is still used today in flashings at the margins of roofs, where they join other walls, chimney-stacks etc. This requires the lead sheeting to be bent into shape, and the harder, more brittle lead is likely to develop cracks and hence leaks. Architects frequently specified that lead to be used on buildings was not to be Ballycorus lead for this reason.

This changed from 1829, when Hugh Lee Pattison in Newcastle-upon-Tyne discovered that when a mixture, or alloy, of lead and silver was melted and allowed to cool slowly the two metals separated. One would crystallise and fall to the bottom of the melting pot, while the

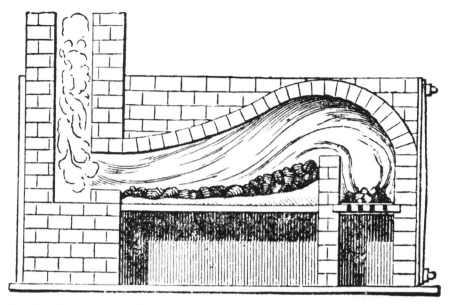

Pl. 57—Reverberatory furnace.

other remained in liquid form. The solid metal was lead and was al-most free from silver, while the liquid was silver. To illustrate the im-pact that this had on the lead and silver industry, imagine lead containing 300 parts per million of silver, or 0.3kg per tonne. Under the original cupellation process, 33 tonnes of lead would have to be cupelled in order to obtain 10kg of silver, while by Pattison's process the whole 10kg is concentrated into one tonne of lead, which alone undergoes cupellation, and the remaining 32 tons have only to be melted again and sent to the market as pure lead.

At the Ballycorus lead works this process took place in a lofty building, open at either end, in which were a series of eight cast-iron cauldrons, set in brick fireplaces. Each cauldron could hold ten tonnes of metal, which was the pig lead that came from the smelting process. A cauldron would be heated until the lead melted and then the heat was reduced a little, until it was just below melt-ing point, and the molten lead began to cool slowly. One of the workers would stir the molten metal with an iron paddle until he could feel from the increased resistance to stirring that some crystals had begun to form at the bottom of the pot. He would then take an immense perforated ladle and sink it to the bottom. A chain attached to the end of the handle of the ladle was drawn in by using a windlass (a form of winch), with the handle of the ladle resting on the side of the cauldron. The lever action raised the perforated ladle up, with the crystals held in the ladle while the molten metal ran through the perforations back into the cauldron. The ladle was shaken to knock any remaining drops of molten metal back into the cauldron. The crystals now contained a lower proportion of silver and were transferred to another cauldron, where the process was repeated. The metal in the original cauldron contained a higher percentage of silver and this was subjected to repetition of the process until the cauldron contained about 8.5kg of silver per tonne. It was not economically viable to continue the process any further to raise the proportion of silver in the mix.

To complete the separation of the silver, the older method of cupellation was used. The cupel, or dish, used for this purpose was made from finely ground bone ash. The furnace had an iron grating on the top; a paste of bone ash and water was pressed onto this grating and shaped into a dish, measuring about 60cm by 45cm. When the cupel was hot, a small amount of molten metal was poured onto it along a narrow channel from a pot in which it had been melted. With the fire raised to its maximum temperature, a strong blast of air was blown over the surface of the molten metal by means of a fan. The hot lead on the surface then reacted with the oxygen in the air to form lead oxide, and this was blown off the surface by the force of the air, 'much as you would blow the froth from a glass of champagne', into a pot. During this process the surface of the metal was extremely bright owing to the intense heat produced by the oxidisation. As the last of the lead was oxidised and blown away, the surface became dull, then suddenly went through a rapid succession of colours until the bright sheet of silver could be seen.

Twenty tonnes of lead were usually cupelled in a single operation, producing a cake of silver weighing about 170kg. In view of the substantial quantity of lead that needed to be processed to produce 170kg of silver, the Pattison process was carried out regularly at the Ballycorus works, while the resulting concentrated mix of lead and silver would be stored until there was twenty tonnes available for cupellation.

Shot-making

The first stage in making lead shot began at the smelting stage, as has been described above. The lead that had been smelted in the blast furnace was brought to a building adjacent to the cupelling house, where there was another furnace. These ingots of lead were

Pl. 58—Riddle house at Ballycorus shot works.

Pl. 59—Grading shot in a riddle house.

darker than the lead smelted in the reverberatory furnace and, being harder, they would make a ringing sound if struck, which normal lead would not do. In this furnace the lead ingots were melted and a small amount of arsenious acid was added. This was the lead that was destined to be converted to lead shot and it needed the traces of arsenic to make it suitable for this purpose. If pure lead is melted and poured through a colander it will form irregularly shaped masses, while lead with a little arsenic in it will produce almost perfect spheres. Only a small quantity of the arsenic is added, amounting to about 7–10 parts per thousand. The resultant mix was known as 'poisoned metal', and on solidifying and cooling it was brought to the shot tower.

The system for making shot has been described in the text above, along with the processes for grading the shot and ensuring that it was spherical.

APPENDIX 3

EMPLOYMENT

It has already been noted that at the outset of its operations in 1826 the company employed 1,400 people, while in later years Knockmahon alone employed 1,200. The numbers would have fluctuated over time, depending on which mines were open and working and what price was being obtained for ore, as at times of low prices the mining operations would often be scaled back. Similarly, the amount of employment at the Ballycorus lead works varied; it was given as forty in 1838, while twenty years or so later, when considering opening a school, the company was informed that a hundred heads of households worked at the plant—implying that others, who may have been sons or brothers of the heads of households, were not included in this number. In 1869 the number employed at the works was given as 66–68.[1] Figures for employment are therefore sketchy and variable.

In January 1855 the chairman informed the shareholders that the company 'employs every day in the year over two thousand five hundred in mere labour, and one thousand children in dressing the ores &c, besides the employment given to mechanics of various denominations'.[2] This figure is not very precise and only gives a minimum number, as it is not clear what constitutes *labour* and who classifies as a *mechanic*. Were miners considered to be just labourers? Does *mechanic* equate to skilled and/or semi-skilled workers, such as those in the lead works? The use of the word *children* is also unclear, as on another occasion, cited below, the chairman stated that females aged between fourteen and twenty were employed; these girls would have been classified as young people and not as children, 'children' being defined in law as those under the age of thirteen.[3]

One question that is frequently asked regarding mines is whether women and children were employed. A parliamentary commission was established in 1841 to investigate the employment of children, and this examined practices throughout the United Kingdom in a range of employment types. The first report of the Children's Employment Commission was published in 1842 and provided the results of its findings in relation to mines.[4] It is worth quoting a range of comments from the report insofar as they relate to mines in Ireland. A number of specific references are made to the Mining Company of Ireland's mines at Luganure, Caime and Knockmahon.

> Page 23—In the coal-mines in the south of Ireland, no children at all were found. All the underground work, which in the coal-mines of England, Scotland and Wales, is done by young children, appears in Ireland to be done by young persons between the ages of thirteen and eighteen.
>
> Page 37—In none of the collieries in the coal fields of Ireland was a single instance found of a female child, or indeed a female of any age, being employed in the coal mines in any kind of underground work.
>
> Page 105—In the collieries of Ireland a few children are

employed as trappers,[5] but none in pushing or drawing coals from the workings to the shafts.

Page 207—In Ireland adult labour is so cheap and
abundant, that children and young persons are employed in far less proportion than in Great Britain.
The following numbers are approximations to accu-
racy:

Wicklow—Avoca copper and sulphur mines, Glenma-
hee [recte Glenmalure?] and Luganure lead mines
and the gold washings[6]—total of work people 2,150;
no children, and few of the young men under eighteen.

Wexford—Caime lead mine; total of work people 127;
7 boys under thirteen, 20 from thirteen to eighteen
and 26 girls between those ages.

Waterford—Knockmahon copper mines; total of work
people 1,100; children employed, though not liked;
young persons also, though number not stated.

Among upwards of 4,500 hands employed in these
mines the proportion under eighteen seems to be
very small.

Page 208—In the mines of [Ireland] there is scarcely an
instance of a child being employed in any kind of
underground work, and even the young men do not
generally enter the mines until approaching adult
age.

Page 229—Surface labour in dressing the ores of tin,
copper, lead and zinc: The proportion of children
employed in this as in many other branches of labour, in Ireland is less than in Great Britain, through
the greater cheapness of adult labour. Girls, however,

are employed as well as boys. The children and young persons are nearly all at the surface; some cobbing, or breaking the ores with a hammer of a size to be received into the crushing machine, and others at the divers operations of washing. Boys sometimes commence work as early as seven or eight years, but generally not until ten, eleven or later; and girls not until eleven, twelve and upwards. Indeed, the managing agent at the Knockmahon Copper Mine objects to the trouble which the children give as almost counterbalancing the value of their labour; alleging that they are most irregular in their attendance, and will not come when the weather is unfavourable, although they work under good wooden sheds.

Pl. 60—Copper mine at Tankardstown, Knockmahon.

Page 232—The washing-grounds of the Irish mines present no peculiarities of character. Sheds are provided in some instances; but generally there is a complete exposure to the weather, against which there is much complaint.

Page 239—Surface labour in dressing the ores of tin, copper, lead and zinc. North Wales (the processes at the Irish mines are precisely similar)—that it is in preparing ore for the smelters that boys are so extensively employed at the mines, and their work is all performed on the surface in the open air. Formerly the boys used to break up the lumps into small fragments by means of hammers; the dust arising from this operation was in part inhaled by them, and produced bad effects, as it tended to induce constipation of the bowels and a peculiar kind of colic, and laid the foundation of many constitutional diseases. At present there are few works in which the ore is not broken by machinery, an improvement which lessens labour and reduces the chances of ill health. When broken, the ore is conveyed by boys to the washing pits and tubs, and by other boys it undergoes several washings through riddles; the parts which contain no metal go off with the water; the lead, on account of its specific gravity, sinks to the bottom of the sieve, and by means of these washings is soon fitted for the smelters.

Page 241—In Ireland the regular hours of work appear to be the same as in England, from six to six in summer, with an hour for dinner and half an hour for breakfast.

Very little information is available in relation to working hours, though local resident Phineas Riall noted that the workers in the smelting works at Ballycorus finished work at 3 o'clock on Saturdays.[7]

> Page 251—The appearance of young people at work on the surface in [Ireland] is described as being generally that of robust health, although they are without shoes or stockings, commonly without any change of clothes, get only two meals of potatoes a day, with sometimes a little buttermilk, and inhabit the wretched cabins which shelter a teeming population even on the sides of the poorest and remotest mountains.

This report was prepared prior to the Great Famine, and it is possible that matters changed in Ireland after that terrible event, as the country was no longer overpopulated to the same extent and labour may not have been as cheap. Nevertheless, the continued high levels of emigration suggest that work remained scarce and hence labour remained cheap.

In 1859 the chairman of the company informed the half-yearly meeting of shareholders that there had been a steady increase in wages paid to those employed at the various mines operated by the company in line with increases in wages all over the country.[8] By way of example, he stated that

> 'The labourers employed in the Knockmahon mines earned wages averaging from 18 to 20 shillings per week, while in the Wicklow and Cork mines the wages were probably two shillings per week less. In addition, there were a

great number of young persons of both sexes employed, who earned each from 9 to 13 pence per day. The people in their employment, he was happy to state, were well re-munerated and in comfortable circumstances.'

In response to this statement, one of the shareholders, James Haughton, asked in what sort of employment the females in the company's service were engaged. The response was that

'the females employed by the company were girls of ages varying from 14 to 20. Their employment was breaking the ore with hammers, separating the stone that contained ore from the portion that did not, and the labour was alto-gether performed out of doors. There were no females em-ployed down in the mines. The captains of the mines told him that there was greater facility in the swing of a girl's arm for the work than was possessed by a man's; whether they would exercise that gift on their husbands was another matter.'

APPENDIX 4

LEAD POISONING

In the late 1830s, when the Ordnance Survey was working on the first-edition six-inch maps, the surveyors recorded that[1]

'the rivers Avonmore and Glendasan abounded some time ago with Trout and Salmon but since the lead mines in Brocca [Glendasan] and Seven Churches [Glendalough] have been opened the mineral waters are said to have killed the fish and also the cattle that drank thereof.'

I assume that the intention was to say that the cattle had drunk the waters, not the fish.

This was not the only comment on the subject. Thirty years later, parliament set up a committee to investigate cattle plague and the resulting report described the symptoms in detail.[2] It noted that some of the symptoms were

'similar in development ... to the slate-coloured margin presented by the gums of persons suffering from chronic lead poisoning, as is frequently observed in house-painters and persons employed in the smelting of lead ore, and has

[19] Griffith, *op. cit.*

[20] Registry of Deeds, book 173, p. 383, no. 116629.

[21] Ball, *op. cit.*, p. 77.

[22] P.S. Kennan, P. McArdle, F.M. Williams and E. Doyle, 'A review of metal deposits associated with the Leinster Granite, SE Ireland, and a model for their genesis', in C.J. Andrew, R.W.A. Crowe, S. Finlay, W.M. Pennell and J.F. Pyne (eds), *Geology and Genesis of Mineral Deposits in Ireland* (Dublin: Irish Association for Economic Geology, 1986), p. 204.

[23] Chris Stillman and George Sevastopulo, *Classic Geology in Europe: Leinster* (Harpenden: Terra Publishing, 2005), p. 133.

[24] Robert Kane, *The Industrial Resources of Ireland* (2nd edn, Dublin: Hodges and Smith, 1845), p. 205.

[25] Registry of Deeds, book 599, p. 237, no. 410965.

[26] W.G. Strickland, *A Dictionary of Irish Artists* (London, 1913; reprinted by Irish Academic Press, 1989), p. 515; 'Hone', in https://dib.cambridge.org (accessed 16 February 2019).

[27] Registry of Deeds, book 735, p. 462, no. 501397.

[28] Registry of Deeds, book 810, p. 105, no. 546040.

3. THE EARLY DAYS AT BALLYCORUS

[1] Diary of Phineas Riall of Old Connaught, 3 January 1844 (private collection).

[2] *Freeman's Journal*, 27 January 1807, p. 3.

[3] Registry of Deeds, book 591, p. 196, no. 402340.

[4] Registry of Deeds, book 591, p. 197, no. 402341.

[5] Registry of Deeds, book 590, p. 534, no. 403946.

[6] *Freeman's Journal*, 7 August 1808, p. 2, and 31 August 1808, p. 1.

[7] *Dublin Journal*, 2 September 1809, p. 2.

[8] *Notes on the Mineralogy of Part of the Vicinity of Dublin, taken principally from the papers of the late Rev Walter Stephens AM* (London, 1812), pp 18–19.

[9] Registry of Deeds, book 697, p. 518, no. 478600, and book 701, p. 389, no. 480878.

[10] *Freeman's Journal*, 24 November 1818, p. 1.

[11] *Freeman's Journal*, 1 March 1819, p. 1.

[12] *Freeman's Journal*, 18 April 1820, p. 1.

[13] Registry of Deeds, book 757, p. 293, no. 514428.

[14] Registry of Deeds, book 761, p. 440, no. 516975.

[15] National Library of Ireland, collection list no. 29, Hibernian Mining Company Papers (MS 29,767).

4. ESTABLISHMENT OF THE MINING COMPANY OF IRELAND

[1] *Reports of the Mining Company of Ireland from April 1824 to December 1854* (Dublin, 1854), p. 5.

[2] Thomas P. Power, *Ministers and Mines—Religious Conflict in an Irish Mining Community, 1847–1858* (Bloomington, Indiana: iUniverse LLC, 2014), p. 27.

[3] *Reports of the Mining Company of Ireland from April 1824 to December 1854*, p. 5.

[4] *Freeman's Journal*, 17 February 1824. Demands for further ten-shilling deposits were made from time to time: e.g. *Freeman's Journal*, 21 October 1824, 21 January 1828, 15 April 1831 and 7 August 1835.

[5] *Mining Company of Ireland, List of Proprietors*, 1824 (NLI ref. ILB P.3001).

[6] *Mining Company of Ireland, List of Proprietors*, 1824 and 1833 (NLI ref. ILB P.3001).

[7] *The Anglo-Celt*, 1 January 1847, p. 7.

[8] Mining Company of Ireland, half-yearly reports, February 1824 and March 1825 (NLI ref. Ir553 m2).

[9] *Belfast Newsletter*, 18 March 1825, p. 2.

[10] MCI, half-yearly report, July 1825.

[11] MCI, half-yearly reports, July 1825, January 1826, July 1826.

[12] National Archives of Ireland, CSO/RP/1828/1562.

[13] National Archives of Ireland, CSO/RP/1828/1845.

[14] *Freeman's Journal*, 22 September 1828, p. 1.

5. THE MINING COMPANY'S ACQUISITION OF BALLYCORUS

[1] Registry of Deeds, book 807, p. 569, no. 544704.

[2] Registry of Deeds, book 822, p. 334, no. 553469.

[3] Registry of Deeds, book 800, p. 229, no. 540164; *Freeman's Journal*, 2 February 1845, p. 3.

[4] Registry of Deeds, book 805, p. 198, no. 543133.

[5] Registry of Deeds, book 876, p. 403, no. 581903.

[6] Ordnance Survey, field name book, parish of Rathmichael, Co. Dublin, 1836.

[7] John Rocque, *An Actual Survey of the County of Dublin* (London, 1760); John Taylor, *A Map of the Environs of Dublin* (Dublin, 1816).

[8] National Library of Ireland, reference 21.F.102 (8).

[9] Robert Kane, *The Industrial Resources of Ireland* (2nd edn, Dublin: Hodges and Smith, 1845), p. 207.

6. THE MINING COMPANY'S FORTUNES

[1] MCI, half-yearly report, 1 December 1826 (NLI ref. Ir553 m2).
[2] MCI, half-yearly reports, July 1825, January 1826, July 1826, January 1827, July 1827.
[3] MCI, half-yearly report, 1 June 1828, appendix—petition to parliament.
[4] *Ibid.*
[5] MCI, half-yearly report, July 1828.
[6] MCI, half-yearly reports, December 1828, June 1829, December 1829, June 1832.
[7] MCI, half-yearly report, December 1832.
[8] Peadar McArdle, *Dissenting Spirit—Thomas Weaver, Geologist and Mining Engineer* (Dublin: The Liffey Press, 2017), p. 173.
[9] MCI, half-yearly reports, June and December 1835.
[10] MCI, half-yearly reports, June and December 1826.
[11] MCI, half-yearly reports, June and December 1837, June and December 1838, June and December 1839.
[12] MCI, half-yearly reports, December 1839, December 1840 (NLI ref. Ir553 m3).
[13] MCI, half-yearly report, 31 May 1851 (NLI ref. Ir553 m3).
[14] MCI, half-yearly reports, December 1852 (NLI ref. Ir553 m3).

7. THE MINING COMPANY AT LUGANURE

[1] Richard Griffith, *Report on the Metallic Mines of the Province of Leinster in Ireland* (Dublin, 1828), p. 13.
[2] Peadar McArdle, *Dissenting Spirit—Thomas Weaver, Geologist and Mining Engineer* (Dublin: The Liffey Press, 2018), pp 117–20.
[3] Donald Stewart, *Report of Donald Stewart, Itinerant Mineralogist to the Dublin Society* (Dublin, 1800), p. 122.
[4] Robert Fraser, *General View of the Agriculture and Mineralogy, Present State and Circumstances of the County Wicklow with some Observations on the Means of their Improvement* (Dublin, 1801), p. 14.
[5] Grenville A.J. Cole, *Memoir of Localities of Minerals of Economic Importance and Metalliferous Mines in Ireland* (Dublin: Geological Survey of Ireland, 1922; republished by the Mining Heritage Society of Ireland, 1998), p. 111; William Fitton (ed.), *Notes on the Mineralogy of part of the Vicinity of Dublin, taken Principally from the Papers of the late Walter Stephens AM* (London, 1812), p. 9.
[6] Registry of Deeds, book 807, p. 569, no. 544704.
[7] *Freeman's Journal*, 12 July 1825.
[8] *Freeman's Journal*, 27 July 1825.
[9] MCI, half-yearly report, July 1825 (NLI ref. Ir553 m2).
[10] MCI half-yearly report, 5 January 1826.
[11] *Freeman's Journal*, 16 August 1825.
[12] Richard Griffith, *Primary Valuation of Tenements*, Derrylossary Parish, Barony of

Ballinacor, North.

13 MCI, half-yearly report, 5 July 1826.

14 MCI, half-yearly report, 1 December 1826.

15 MCI, half-yearly report, 1 June 1827.

16 Ordnance Survey, 1838, Wicklow sheet 23.

17 MCI, half-yearly report, 1 May 1831, *Reports of the Mining Company of Ireland from April 1824 to December 1854* (Dublin: John Porteous, 1855).

18 MCI, half-yearly report, 1 December 1828, *Reports of the Mining Company of Ireland from April 1824 to December 1854.*

19 MCI, half-yearly report, 1 December 1830.

20 MLI, half-yearly reports, 1830–4.

21 MLI, half-yearly reports, June and December 1835, *Reports of the Mining Company of Ireland from April 1824 to December 1854.*

22 MLI, half-yearly reports, June and December 1836, *Reports of the Mining Company of Ireland from April 1824 to December 1854.*

23 MLI, half-yearly reports, 1837–9, *Reports of the Mining Company of Ireland from April 1824 to December 1854.*

24 MLI, half-yearly reports, 1840–5, *Reports of the Mining Company of Ireland from April 1824 to December 1854.*

25 Robert Kane, *The Industrial Resources of Ireland* (2nd edn, Dublin: Hodges and Smith, 1845), p. 206.

26 MCI, half-yearly report, 31 May 1851 (NLI ref. Ir622 m3).

27 MCI, half-yearly report, 31 May 1850 (NLI ref. Ir622 m3).

28 MCI, half-yearly report, 31 May 1851 (NLI ref. Ir622 m3).

29 B. Symons, 'Luganure Lead Mines, Co. Wicklow', *The Dublin Builder*, 15 December 1866, p. 293.

30 MCI, half-yearly reports, 1850–70 (NLI ref. Ir622 m3), and as reported in the *Dublin Builder* and the *Irish Times*.

8. THE MINING COMPANY AT BALLYCORUS

1 Registry of Deeds, book 800, p. 229, no. 540164.

2 *Freeman's Journal*, 27 July 1825; MCI, half-yearly report, July 1825 (NLI ref. Ir553 m2).

3 MCI, half-yearly report, July 1825 (NLI ref. Ir553 m2).

4 Rob Goodbody, *Dún Laoghaire–Rathdown Industrial Heritage Survey* (Dún Laoghaire–Rathdown County Council, 2006).

5 *Freeman's Journal*, 6 August 1825.

6 MCI, half-yearly report, 5 January 1826.

7 *Ibid.*

8 MCI, half-yearly report, 5 July 1826.

9 MCI, half-yearly report, 1 June 1827.

10 MCI, half-yearly reports, 1 June and 31 December 1828.

[11] MCI, half-yearly report, 1 June 1829; Registry of Deeds, book 849, p. 305, no. 568305.

[12] MCI, half-yearly report, 1 June 1830.

[13] MCI, half-yearly report, December 1832.

[14] MCI, half-yearly report, June 1832.

[15] MCI, half-yearly report, June 1833.

[16] MCI, half-yearly reports, December 1834 and June 1835.

[17] MCI, half-yearly report, December 1835.

[18] MCI, half-yearly report, December 1836.

[19] *Ibid.*

[20] Lt. George A. Bennett, RE, Ordnance Survey field name book, parish of Rathmichael, Co. Dublin, November 1836; typed transcript in NLI, ref. BB6445, p. 47.

[21] Ordnance Survey six-inch map of County Dublin, sheet 26 (1843).

[22] John D'Alton, *The History of the County of Dublin* (Dublin: Hodges and Smith, 1838), p. 925.

[23] MCI, half-yearly reports, 1836 and 1837.

[24] MCI, half-yearly reports, 1 June and 1 December 1839.

[25] MCI, half-yearly reports, 1 June and 1 December 1840.

[26] *Freeman's Journal*, 2 July 1858.

[27] MCI, half-yearly reports, 1837 to 1840.

[28] MCI, half-yearly reports, 1841 to 1849.

[29] *Freeman's Journal*, 6 January 1843.

[30] *Freeman's Journal*, 7 January 1848.

[31] Chairman's address to half-yearly meeting of the Mining Company of Ireland, 1 July 1858, as reported in the *Freeman's Journal*, 2 July 1858.

[32] MCI, half-yearly reports, 1846 to 1853.

[33] Richard Griffith, *Primary Valuation of Tenements*, Rathmichael Parish, Barony of Rathdown, August 1848.

[34] Ordnance Survey six-inch map of County Dublin, sheet 26 (1843).

[35] Robert Kane, *The Industrial Resources of Ireland* (2nd edn, Dublin: Hodges and Smith, 1845), p. 216.

[36] *Ibid.*, p. 218.

9. THE RECONSTRUCTION OF BALLYCORUS

[1] Registry of Deeds, 1853, book 4, no. 291.

[2] Registry of Deeds, 1853, book 4, no. 292.

[3] Valuation Office, cancelled books, parish of Rathmichael, Co. Dublin, townland of Ballycorus, plot 2, 'Mines reopened in June 1853 and therefore not liable to be rated until June 1860—the buildings and land only are valued now. By order of General Superintendent, 12th December 1853'.

[4] MCI, half-yearly reports, 1853 to 1860.

[5] MCI, half-yearly report, December 1860.

[6] *Freeman's Journal*, 4 January 1856.

[7] *The Nation*, 12 July 1856.

[8] MCI, half-yearly reports, 1853 to 1861.

[9] *Freeman's Journal*, 3 July 1857.

[10] Registry of Deeds, 1857, book 58, no. 226.

[11] *Irish Times*, 6 July 1860.

[12] *Dublin Builder*, 15 January 1863, p. 11.

[13] *Irish Times*, 6 July 1860.

[14] MCI, half-yearly report, *Irish Times*, 6 July 1860.

[15] MCI, half-yearly reports, 1861 to 1863.

[16] MCI, half-yearly report, *Dublin Builder*, 15 July 1864, p. 138.

[17] *Waterford News and Star*, 10 January 1862.

[18] Diary of Phineas Riall of Old Connaught, 14 October 1860 and 3 July 1861 (private collection).

[19] There are videos available on YouTube showing the steeplejack Fred Dibnah at work, climbing high chimneys, erecting scaffolding and carrying out repairs. These should not be watched by anyone who has no head for heights.

[20] I am very grateful to Dr Craig Meskell, Associate Professor of Mechanical and Manufacturing Engineering in Trinity College, Dublin, for kindly supplying the explanations in relation to helical strakes, vortex shedding, the Bunsen effect and air flow in general.

[21] Seán J. White, 'A South Dublin tower', in *Our Lady of the Wayside National School, Kilternan—silver jubilee, 1965–1990* (published by the school, 1990).

[22] National Archives of Ireland, Valuation house book, parish of Rathmichael, Co. Dublin, ref. O.L. 5.0924.

[23] MCI, half-yearly report, July 1859.

[24] *Irish Times*, 5 July 1861.

[25] *Waterford News and Star*, 10 January 1862.

[26] *Freeman's Journal*, 3 July 1857.

[27] *The Nation*, 29 August 1858.

[28] www.dia.ie, accessed 30 December 2018.

[29] Institution of Mechanical Engineers visit to Ballycorus, *Freeman's Journal*, 2 August 1865.

[30] J. Beete Jukes and G.V. Du Noyer, *Explanations to accompany Sheets 121 and 130 of the Maps of the Geological Survey of Ireland illustrating a portion of the Counties of Wicklow and Dublin* (Commissioners of Her Majesty's Treasury, 1869), p. 44.

[31] *Freeman's Journal*, 8 July 1859; *Irish Times*, 6 July 1860.

[32] *Freeman's Journal*, 6 July 1860; B.J. Lewis, J.M. Cimbala and A.M. Wouden, 'Major historical developments in the design of water wheels and Francis hydroturbines', *IOP Conference Series: Earth and Environment Science* 22 (2014).

[33] MCI, half-yearly report, 30 June 1861; *Irish Times*, 5 July 1861.

[34] *Irish Times*, 5 July 1961.

[35] Joseph Mills, *Recollections of Shankill during the 'Reign' of the Exterminator, Sir Charles Domvile* (Shankill, 1906).

[36] Valuation Office, cancelled books, parish of Kilternan, Co. Dublin.

[37] *Dublin Builder*, 15 July 1862, and various entries for Charles Geoghegan.

[38] Irish Architectural Archive, Charles Geoghegan Drawings, 80/32 D.6.

[39] Valuation Office, cancelled books, Rathmichael parish, Ballycorus townland, plot number 3A, 1884.

[40] *Irish Times*, 22 July 1881.

[41] *Irish Times*, 5 November 1883.

[42] Valuation Office, cancelled books, Rathmichael parish, Ballycorus townland, plot number 7A, 1884 and 1915.

[43] Ernie Shepherd and Gerry Beesley, *Dublin and South Eastern Railway* (Leicester: Midland Publishing Ltd, 1998), p. 18.

[44] 'Application ... for the making of a new road twenty-five feet in the clear ... two hundred and twenty-seven perches long ...', NLI, Domvile papers, MS 11776.

[45] NLI Domvile papers, MS 11776.

[46] *Freeman's Journal*, 30 October 1867.

[47] *Irish Times*, 2 November 1881.

[48] Mary Mulvihill, *Ingenious Ireland* (Dublin: Town House, 2002), pp 186–7.

[49] Liam Clare, *The Bray and Enniskerry Railway* (Stroud: Nonsuch Publishing, 2007), pp 53–4.

[50] Griffith's Valuation, Rathmichael parish, Co. Dublin, townlands of Rathmichael and Ballycorus, 1848.

[51] Valuation Office, cancelled books, Rathmichael parish, Co. Dublin, townlands of Rathmichael and Ballycorus, 1855.

[52] MCI, half-yearly report, 27 December 1860.

[53] Valuation Office, cancelled books, Rathmichael parish, Ballycorus townland.

[54] Valuation Office, cancelled books, Rathmichael parish, Ballycorus townland

[55] Mills, *Recollections of Shankill*.

[56] File on Ballycorus male and female schools, National Archives of Ireland, ref. ED/1/30/22.

[57] *Dublin Builder*, 1 November 1860, p. 361; G.O. Simms, *Tullow's Story—A Portrait of a County Dublin Parish* (Select Vestry of Tullow Parish, 1983), p. 41.

[58] www.dia.ie (accessed 31 December 2018); Frederick O'Dwyer, 'The architecture of the Board of Public Works 1831–1823', in Ciaran O'Connor and John O'Regan (eds), *Public Works—the Architecture of the Office of Public Works 1831–1987* (Dublin: Architectural Association of Ireland, 1987).

[59] Files on Ballycorus male and female schools, National Archives of Ireland, ref. ED/1/30/22 and ED/1/30/73.

[60] MCI, half-yearly meeting, 3 July 1862; *Irish Times*, 4 July 1862.

[61] *Our Lady of the Wayside National School, Kilternan—silver jubilee, 1965–1990* (published by the school, 1990), pp 41 and 43.

[62] *Second Report of the Commissioners on Education Inquiry* (1826), pp 842–3.

[63] MCI, half-yearly meeting, *Irish Times*, 2 January 1863.

[64] *Dublin Builder*, 1 May 1864, p. 67.

[65] *Thirtieth Report of the Commissioners of National Education in Ireland for the year*

1863, House of Commons Papers (1864), p. 151.

[66] *Thirty-first Report of the Commissioners of National Education in Ireland for the year 1864*, House of Commons Papers (1865), p. 155.

[67] *Irish Times*, 8 July 1864.

[68] *Irish Times*, 6 January 1865.

[69] *Freeman's Journal*, 7 January 1865.

[70] The last manager of the lead works at Ballycorus was a Robert Roberts. He was born in County Wicklow but would only have been about three years old at the time these awards were made.

[71] *Thirty-sixth Report of the Commissioners of National Education in Ireland for the year 1869*, House of Commons Papers (1870), pp 557 and 596.

[72] Valuation Office, cancelled books, electoral district of Brockagh, County Wicklow, Seven Churches townland, plot 3b.

[73] *Irish Times*, 8 September 1994.

10. MINING AND PROCESSING

[1] B. McConnell, *Geology of Kildare–Wicklow* (Geological Survey of Ireland, n.d.).

[2] Robert Kane, *The Industrial Resources of Ireland* (2nd edn, Dublin: Hodges and Smith, 1845), p. 206.

[3] Ernie Shepherd and Gerry Beesley, *Dublin and South Eastern Railway* (Leicester: Midland Publishing Ltd, 1998), p. 18.

[4] Kane, *op. cit.*, p. 216.

11. LUGANURE FROM 1860 ONWARD

[1] *Freeman's Journal*, 6 January 1854.

[2] Samuel Haughton, *Notes on Irish Mines—No. II. Lead Mines of Luganure, County of Wicklow* (Dublin: Gill, 1855), p. 5.

[3] *Cork Examiner*, 10 July 1855.

[4] *Freeman's Journal*, 4 January 1856.

[5] *Ibid.*

[6] *Freeman's Journal*, 2 January 1857.

[7] *Freeman's Journal*, 2 January and 3 July 1857.

[8] *Freeman's Journal*, 3 July 1857.

[9] *Freeman's Journal*, 3 July 1863.

[10] Valuation Office, cancelled books, electoral district of Brockagh, County Wicklow, townland of Seven Churches; Ordnance Survey six-inch map, Wicklow sheet 23 (1887).

[11] *Irish Times*, 6 January 1860; *Freeman's Journal*, 6 July 1860.

[12] Valuation Office, cancelled books, electoral district of Brockagh, County Wicklow, townland of Seven Churches; Joan Kavanagh (ed.), *The Glen of the Two Lakes—Glendalough, a Pictorial History* (Glendalough: Wicklow Rural Partnership Ltd, 2003),

p. 171.

[13] Irish Architectural Archive, Charles Geoghegan collection, 80/32, D.1 to D.5.

[14] *Irish Times*, 4 July 1862.

[15] *Cork Examiner*, 11 January 1854.

[16] *Waterford News and Star*, 10 January 1862.

[17] *Irish Times*, 3 July 1868.

[18] *Irish Times*, 7 January 1870.

[19] Based on spot heights marked on the first-edition Ordnance Survey map.

[20] *Irish Times*, 7 January 1870, 8 July 1870 and 6 January 1871.

[21] *Irish Times*, 6 July 1871.

[22] *Irish Times*, 7 July 1871, 5 July 1872 and 17 January 1873; *Freeman's Journal*, 5 January 1872, 17 January 1873 and 18 July 1873.

[23] *Irish Times*, 7 July 1875.

12. BALLYCORUS FROM THE 1860s

[1] *Freeman's Journal*, 7 July 1865.

[2] Parke Neville, 'Dublin Waterworks', *Civil Engineer and Architects' Journal*, vol. 28 (1865), p. 266.

[3] *Irish Times*, report of half-yearly meeting, 5 July 1866.

[4] *Irish Times*, report on half-yearly meeting, 4 January 1867.

[5] *The Irish Builder*, 1 March 1873, p. 71.

[6] *The Irish Builder*, 1 June 1873, p. 158.

[7] *Freeman's Journal*, 2 July 1869.

[8] *Irish Times*, 8 July 1870.

[9] *Irish Times*, 6 January 1871.

[10] *Freeman's Journal*, 5 January 1872.

[11] *Freeman's Journal*, 18 July 1873.

[12] *Freeman's Journal*, 16 January 1874.

[13] *Irish Times*, 22 January and 7 July 1875.

13. THE MINING COMPANY FROM THE 1850s

[1] This section is largely based on the Mining Company's half-yearly reports to its shareholders and the reports of shareholders' meetings, as reported in the *Irish Times*, the *Freeman's Journal*, the *Dublin Builder* and the *Irish Builder*.

[2] *Irish Times*, 2 January 1863.

[3] F.G. Hall, *History of the Bank of Ireland* (Dublin: Hodges Figgis, 1949), pp 245–7.

[4] *Irish Times*, 4 January 1867.

[5] *Ibid.*

[6] *Dublin Builder*, 15 January 1866, pp 27–8.

[7] Steve Fletcher, 'Lead mining in Spain in the 19th century: Spanish industry or British adventure?', *Bulletin of the Peak District Mines Historical Society*, vol. 11, no. 4 (1991), p.

195.

8 J. Beete Jukes and G.V. Du Noyer, *Explanations to accompany Sheets 121 and 130 of the Maps of the Geological Survey of Ireland illustrating a portion of the Counties of Wicklow and Dublin* (Commissioners of Her Majesty's Treasury, 1869), p. 44.

9 Fletcher, *op. cit.*, p. 196.

10 *Irish Times*, 16 January and 7 July 1880.

11 'The condition of mining in Ireland', *Irish Times*, 2 February 1882.

12 Joseph Byrne, *Byrne's Dictionary of Irish Local History* (Cork: Mercier Press, 2004), p. 66.

13 *Irish Times*, 16 July 1880.

14 *Irish Times*, 22 July 1881.

15 *Irish Times*, 20 January 1882.

16 *Irish Times*, 9 January 1883.

17 *Freeman's Journal*, 17 July 1885.

18 *Cork Examiner*, 8 July 1886.

19 *Freeman's Journal*, 21 January 1887.

20 *Freeman's Journal*, 18 January 1889.

21 *Freeman's Journal*, 10 July 1889.

22 *Irish Times*, 23 August 1889.

23 Culm is coal dust that is of low value but may be compressed to form it into cakes to be burned like briquettes.

24 *Irish Times*, report of half-yearly meeting, 18 July 1890, and advertisement for sale, 25 July 1890.

25 *Irish Times*, 16 January 1891.

26 Registry of Deeds, 1891, book 36, no. 130, and 1891, book 36, no. 131.

27 *Irish Times*, 27 August 1891.

28 Chris Stillman and George Sevastopulo, *Classic Geology in Europe 6—Leinster* (Harpendon: Terra Publishing, 2005), p. 133.

14. THE NEW COMPANY AT BALLYCORUS

1 *The Industries of Dublin* (London, n.d.), p. 90.

2 *Thom's Directory*, various dates.

3 *Freeman's Journal*, 28 August 1856; *Thom's Directory*, 1857.

4 *Freeman's Journal*, 4 January 1869.

5 *Irish Times*, 22 December 1884.

6 *The Industries of Dublin*, p. 61.

7 *Cork Examiner*, 2 April 1904.

8 George Valentine Roberts, *1893—The Years Between—1983* (privately published, 1983), p. 6.

9 *Thom's Directory*, 1917.

EPILOGUE

1. Valuation Office, cancelled books, electoral district of Brockagh, County Wicklow. The Valuation Office inspectors noted the change of owner to Wyndham H. Wynne in 1891, while Albert A. Wynne was added in the following year.
2. House of Commons Papers [C.6657], *Mines and Minerals—Mineral Statistics of the United Kingdom of Great Britain and Ireland, with the Isle of Man, for the year 1891*, (London and Dublin, 1892), p. 108.
3. House of Commons Papers [C.7024], *Mines and Minerals—Mineral Statistics of the United Kingdom of Great Britain and Ireland, with the Isle of Man, for the year 1892* (London and Dublin, 1893–4), p. 65.
4. *Irish Independent*, 15 March 1921.
5. Wicklow Rural Partnership Ltd and Keith Malone Video Productions, *The Life and Times of Glendalough Mines* (DVD, 2006).
6. *Evening Herald*, 2 October 1935.
7. *Cork Examiner, Irish Independent* and *Evening Herald*, various dates in September and October 1935.
8. *Irish Times*, 2 August 1943.
9. Joan Kavanagh (ed.), *The Glen of the Two Lakes—Glendalough, a Pictorial History* (Glendalough: Wicklow Rural Partnership Ltd, 2003), p. 168.
10. *Irish Times*, 6 September 1956.
11. *Irish Independent*, 8 January 1957.
12. *Evening Herald*, 11 April 1957.
13. *The Life and Times of Glendalough Mines* (DVD).
14. William Dick, pers. comm.; William walked through the mountain in his youth.
15. *Hansard*, written answers (Commons) of Tuesday 25 April 1916.
16. *Hansard*, Commons sitting of Monday 16 July 1917.
17. Planning files in Dublin County Council, investigated by the author in the 1980s; *Irish Times*, 11 January 1958, p. 11.
18. My thanks to the late Howard McConnell for giving me the opportunity to view this while it was visible.
19. https://www.duedil.com/company/ie/1538/the-mining-company-of-ireland-and-strachan-brothers-limited (accessed 7 January 2020).

APPENDIX 2: PROCESSES

1. Harry Napier Draper, 'Lead in two parts—part I, the mouth of the mine; part II, in the furnace', *Recreative Science*, vol. 1 (1860).
2. Brendan O'Donoghue, *The Irish County Surveyors 1834–1944, a Biographical Dictionary* (Dublin: Four Courts Press, 2007), p. 158.
3. Draper, *op. cit.*, pp 289–92.
4. Samuel Haughton, *Notes on Irish Mines—No. II. Lead Mines of Luganure, County of Wicklow* (Dublin: Gill, 1855), p. 4.

⁵ This inclined plane ran from high up on Camaderry Mountain on the northern side of the valley of Glendalough and pre-dated the one constructed from Van Diemen's Land in 1869–70.

⁶ Draper, *op. cit.*, pp 349–53.

APPENDIX 3: EMPLOYMENT

¹ J. Beete Jukes and G.V. Du Noyer, *Explanations to accompany Sheets 121 and 130 of the Maps of the Geological Survey of Ireland illustrating a portion of the Counties of Wicklow and Dublin* (Commissioners of Her Majesty's Treasury, 1869), p. 44.

² *Freeman's Journal*, 5 January 1855.

³ 4 William IV, c.1, section II.

⁴ *Children's Employment Commission, first report of the Commissioners—Mines*, House of Commons Papers, 380, 381 and 382 (1842).

⁵ Some coal mines had trapdoors to regulate ventilation. Trappers were responsible for opening and closing these trapdoors, particularly to allow wagons to pass.

⁶ 'Gold washings' refers to panning for gold in the Goldmine River, south of Woodenbridge.

⁷ Diary of Phineas Riall of Old Connaught, 28 September 1867 (private collection).

⁸ *Freeman's Journal*, 7 January 1859.

APPENDIX 4: LEAD POISONING

¹ Ordnance Survey Name Books, Derrybawn townland, parish of Derry Lossary, Co. Wicklow, vol. 2 (NLI ref. Ir 92942 O3, No. 140).

² *Sequel to the Report of the Committee Convened by the Lord Lieutenant of Ireland to Consider the Measures to be Adopted for Arresting the Progress of the Cattle Plague, in Case of its Appearance in Ireland* (Dublin, 1866), p. 26.

³ Charles Cameron, *Lectures on the Preservation of Health* (London and New York, 1868), p. 67.

⁴ *Dublin Builder*, 1 October 1863, p. 166; 1 August 1864, p. 152.

⁵ *Irish Builder*, 1 December 1886, p. 324; 1 February 1890, p. 40; 1 February 1893, p. 35.

⁶ George Valentine Roberts, *1893—The Years Between—1983* (privately published, 1983), p. 9.

⁷ *Irish Times*, 31 August 2005, p. 13.

INDEX

THE AUTHOR

Rob Goodbody is a building historian. His primary degree included the study of geology, archaeology and historical geography, and he holds masters' degrees in building conservation and local history. He was a founding member of both the Mining Heritage Trust of Ireland and the Industrial Heritage Association of Ireland and has been on the committee of the Rathmichael Historical Society since 1984.

Previous books include *Sir Charles Domvile and his Shankill Estate*; *The Metals—From Dalkey to Dun Laoghaire*; *Irish Historic Towns Atlas, Dublin, Part III—1756– 1847*; and *On the Borders of the Pale—A History of the Kilgobbin, Stepaside and Sandyford Area*. He has also co-authored a number of books, including *The Martello Towers of Dublin* and *Dublin Bay—Nature and History*, and edited the second edition of *Irish Stone Bridges* by Peter O'Keeffe and Tom Simington.